MW00559537

Bake Smart

Bake Smart

Sweets and Secrets from My Oven to Yours

Samantha Seneviratne

HARVEST

An Imprint of WILLIAM MORROW

For my palimy

Contents

Recipes

Here's a more traditional table of contents, just in case this would be helpful too.

CORE RECIPES

COOKIES & BARS

CAKES

Introduction

Every day at around 4:30 p.m., I hear the *clomp clomp* of my five-year-old son Artie's footsteps as he comes up the stairs with our beloved nanny, Zaii. Once he gets through the door, he usually forgets the "shoes off and wash hands" rule, sprints down the hallway, and jumps triumphantly into my arms. He's a string bean of a boy, and if the size of his feet is any indication, he'll soon be as tall as I am, but that doesn't stop me from picking him up and squeezing him for as long as he'll let me.

One afternoon not long ago, I was working on recipes for this book. I do a lot of recipe developing at home for various projects, publications, and websites, and it can be tricky to work solo, without a team of trusted colleagues to taste each pass as I had when I worked as a magazine food editor. That day, I had spent hours trying to develop a yeasted rugelach cookie. I wanted soft and chewy, but also flaky in the right places, with a smooth, rich chocolatey filling that didn't ooze out. This was proving more difficult than expected. The texture was wrong. The filling spilled out in the oven. The size was off, heavy and huge. The kitchen was covered in a layer of sticky goo and the sink looked like a Jenga tournament. Days like these make me question my career.

When I hugged Artie that afternoon, he peeked over my shoulder and asked what I had made. "A mess," I said. "Just a big mess." He asked

if he could try a cookie. You should know that Artie is generally not a huge fan of my cooking. He'll choose a lollipop over pretty much anything I bake. But this time he was interested. He grabbed a particularly doughy specimen and took a bite. His big brown eyes lit up. He gobbled it down and asked for another. Later, as I was working through the pile of dishes in the sink, he snuck in and took another rugelach.

You won't find that particular recipe in this book—I never even wrote it up. But I did learn something from it. In the process of trying to make the ideal cookie, I had forgotten something crucial. I had tinkered with the sugar, the flour, the filling, the oven temperature, and the baking time. But really only one standard matters: Homemade desserts are supposed to make people happy. A cookie is meant for pleasure. That's the point of making something from scratch and sharing it. Not the perfect texture, shape, size, or looks, but joy. And love. And happiness. We should bake for fun and to make (and eat) delicious things. And that's what this book is about.

So often people tell me that they're intimidated by baking—that it seems too complicated, strict, and unforgiving. I understand completely. Most of us don't bake as often as we cook. And baking involves different processes than cooking. For one thing, it's not as simple to change course midstream if something doesn't look quite right. But that doesn't mean baking has to be hard, complicated, or scientifically precise to laboratory levels. Let's give ourselves a break!

Cooking has rules. You wouldn't try to cook rice without any liquid. You wouldn't throw salmon in boiling water and hope for the best. You wouldn't microwave an egg in its shell. In that way, baking is the same. There are some fundamentals, but beyond that, you're free to experiment and create. And once the fundamentals are in place, even mistakes usually taste pretty good.

Contrary to many of the rules that have been passed down across the generations, baking can also be improvised. It should be. That's what I do every time I develop a recipe. For example, let's say I want to create a new loaf cake. I might start with a recipe I've developed for a classic pound cake. Then I consider all the different characteristics of the loaf cake I want and adjust the pound cake recipe accordingly. Maybe I want a finer crumb, so I swap out some confectioners' sugar for some of the granulated. Or maybe I want a browner crust, so I tinker with the leavening and the dairy. I bake what I want to eat, whatever I think will bring me and the people I love the most happiness and joy.

You should be able to bake what you want too, and I want to help you do that. My goal in writing this book was to lay out some of the essentials and encourage my readers to create their own dream desserts. In each chapter, I focus on an important ingredient and share some best practices for working with it. The "core recipes," which include such basics as a laminated butter pastry dough, caramel sauce, and the perfect custard, are meant to exemplify those techniques, to help explain more fundamentals visually, and to give you the opportunity to exercise your skills. The recipes that follow then use those core recipes and the highlighted chapter ingredient so that you can practice what you've learned with confidence. I also included other things I think you really need to know, dispelling some myths, uncomplicating some techniques, and, hopefully, bringing pure joy and breezy simplicity back to the art of everyday baking. Baking takes time, but it doesn't have to be hard. I want to empower you to create, improvise, and improve—and to avoid getting tripped up by old rules that aren't actually so important.

There are already plenty of how-to-bake books. This is not one of those. I want to tell you some of the things that no one else has ever told you about baking, the secrets I tell my friends: Don't bother sifting flour. Don't worry about tiny streaks of egg yolk in your whites when you separate the eggs for the mini pavlovas on page 100. And, most important, know that imperfect cookies can still be delicious.

I hope to take some of the pressure off and guide you toward whatever form of happiness and joy you want to eat and share with your beloveds. Let's bake smart, not hard. Let's bake together.

Big, Fluffy Lemon and
Orange Buns (page 210)

Butter

Before I could find it in New York, I used to pack my suitcase full of perfect golden bars of Le Beurre Bordier, my all-time favorite butter, on trips back from France. Once I realized that the cargo hold of a plane was cold enough to whiz five pounds of heaven over the Atlantic, I took full advantage. Le Beurre Bordier comes in petite 125 gram blocks wrapped in pretty white paper that crinkles seductively as you unfold it. My favorite version has crunchy crystals of fleur de sel nestled throughout. When stirred into chocolate chip cookie dough, it adds the softest, sweetest dairy essence, just milky enough but also slightly savory. The butter isn't just fat here. It's flavor. And it helps coax out the best of the vanilla, the salt, and the chocolate.

Butter isn't the only fat in my sweet kitchen, but it's absolutely my favorite. I believe it's also the ingredient that can have the most interesting results in baked goods, if you know how to manipulate it.

Butter Basics

All butters are made of milk solids, water, and at least 80 percent milk fat (that's the tasty stuff). European butters generally have a bit more fat—somewhere between 82 and 88 percent. The higher fat content usually comes with a higher price tag. I decide which butter to use based on the butter's role in the final product. European butter is great, especially in a laminated dough or a rich buttercream frosting, where its flavor is on display, but ordinary American butter will always be just fine there as well, and everywhere else. Use what you have. Use what you can find easily. Don't stress.

You will have to decide between salted and unsalted butter. The age-old baker's rule is to use unsalted butter, so that you have more control over the amount of salt in the recipe. I think that's an outdated approach, and that salted butter is just fine in baked goods. The amount of added salt in a stick of salted butter is not going to ruin anything, and in some cases (hello, cookies!), salted butter actually works better. (I asked the recipe testers and food stylists who worked on the recipes in this book to use salted butter and unsalted butter interchangeably without thinking about it too much. Either way, we were always happy with the results!) I think it's the quality of the butter, not the salt content, that makes the biggest difference.

I suggest you simply use the same butter you would use on your toast in your baking projects. If you like the taste of it there, you'll like it in your cakes too.

Butter and Temperature

The way that butter is incorporated into a recipe, whether it be creamed with sugar, laminated, or melted, has a considerable effect on the outcome. Cold butter cut into pie pastry or rolled into sheets between layers of dough in laminated pastry will melt in the heat of the oven and create steam, which will puff up the dough and create flakes and layers. Creaming sugar into room-temperature butter results in little air bubbles that will expand in the oven to create lift. Melted butter incorporated into a dough will coat the proteins in the flour and inhibit the formation of gluten. This will create "short," or tender, crumbly pastry, like in the perfect shortbread cookie.

Temperature Matters

Cold	Butter right from the fridge will be below 50°F. If you touch a stick of cold butter with a fingertip, it should not leave a mark.
Room Temperature	At about 65°F, butter will be soft and pliable, but not greasy. If you can bend a stick without smooshing it, it is at room temperature.
Softened	At about 75°F, butter will be shiny and very soft.
Melted	Butter melts at about 105°F; for most recipes, it should then be cooled slightly, to about 90°F, before using.

How to Soften Butter Quickly

To achieve room-temperature or softened butter in a flash, use the microwave: Stand the cold sticks, still wrapped, up on their ends. Heat the butter in 6- to 8-second bursts, flipping the sticks over onto the other end after each burst. Within 18 to 24 seconds or so, the butter should be at room temperature. Add another burst or two for softened butter. Note that this trick applies only to butter that is wrapped in paper. Do not try this with sticks wrapped in foiled paper.

Storing Butter

Store butter in the coldest part of the fridge, not the butter keeper in the fridge door; well wrapped, it should keep for at least a month. But give it a sniff if you have any doubt; you'll know immediately if it's off or has absorbed unpleasant flavors or aromas. I prefer not to freeze butter, as sometimes the texture changes slightly on thawing.

Rolling Out Pastry Dough 101

1. Use a light hand with the flour. Too much flour will lead to tough dough.

2. The dough should be cold enough that it's not sticky, *but* it must be warm enough to roll out without cracking. It's a delicate balance. You can smack cold dough with a rolling pin a few times to warm it up or let it stand at room temperature for a few minutes. Just be sure to rotate the dough between whaps so that you don't thin it out or crack it.

3. Roll the disk of dough from the middle outward, stopping about 1 inch shy of the edge, then rotate it about 45 degrees and roll it out again. Never roll the pin over the edge of the dough—that leads to skinny edges and a thick middle. Rotating the dough often ensures that it doesn't get stuck to the work surface. But when it does stick, run a large offset spatula under the dough to release it, adding a little more flour as necessary.

4. If you're at all nervous, or it's a hot day, roll the dough out on a piece of floured parchment. That way, if the dough gets too warm and starts sticking, you can easily transfer the whole thing to a baking sheet and pop it into the fridge for a rest.

Creaming Butter and Sugar

I don't look at the clock for this step, although most recipes, including mine, include time markers as a guide. The result depends on what kind of mixer you're using and how warm your butter is. Better to look at the color and texture of the butter-sugar mixture and use the time indicators as general guidelines.

DEEP YELLOW: Still the color of uncreamed butter. Not there yet.
PALE YELLOW: Just right. The mixture should also be fluffy, but it can become fluffy before it's fully creamed, so check the color too.
WHITE: Too far. Obviously, there is nowhere to go at this point. Honestly, though, you're not going to destroy your cake by using a white mixture, but always try to stop before you get here. Overwhipped butter can lead to crumbly cakes.

Laminated Butter Pie Pastry

MAKES ENOUGH DOUGH FOR 1 SINGLE PIECRUST

Jam-packed with butter, this flavorful crust will become your go-to. It's not quite puff pastry, but it's not far off. The dough is rolled and folded—i.e., laminated—to build up strength in the pastry and to press the butter into flat sheets. Then, when the butter melts in the oven, it creates steam that will puff up the dough. "Flaky" doesn't even begin to cover it.

You can bake this dough in a pie plate or tart pan, or without using a vessel at all. (Unlike the Tender Free-form Galette Dough, page 6, which is best used, well, free-form.)

- 1¼ cups (170 grams) all-purpose flour
- 2 teaspoons granulated sugar
- ½ teaspoon kosher salt
- 8 tablespoons (1 stick; 113 grams) cold butter, cut into pieces
- ¼ cup (60 grams) ice water, plus more if needed

Using ice water helps ensure that the butter stays cold. Just make sure that little pieces of ice don't end up in the dough. They will melt in the oven and could create holes in the crust. I like to use those big blocks of ice usually designated for cocktails to avoid that problem.

The copious amount of fat and the little bit of sugar also facilitate surface browning, which adds new and complex flavors to the baked pastry.

I think piecrusts benefit from salted butter, which gives them an almost savory edge.

In a large bowl, mix together the flour, sugar, and salt. Add the butter and toss to combine, then smoosh each of the butter pieces flat between your fingers. Make a well in the center of the flour-butter mixture and add the water. Toss with a fork to combine. If everything is evenly moistened and you can press the crumbs together at this point, you don't need more water. If you do need more, add it a teaspoon or two at a time. Tip the dough out, form it into a square, wrap in plastic wrap, and chill until cold, at least 1 hour.

On a lightly floured surface with a floured rolling pin, roll the dough out into a large rectangle about ¼ inch thick with a short side parallel to the edge of the work surface. Fold the top third of the dough down over the middle third of the dough and then fold the bottom third up over that. Wrap the dough well in plastic wrap and chill for about 30 minutes. Repeat the rolling and folding process one more time. Wrap the dough again and chill for at least 1 hour before using.

The dough can be stored, well wrapped, for up to 2 days in the refrigerator or 1 month in the freezer. Let frozen dough thaw in the fridge before using.

Smooshing the butter into flakes flattens the pieces of butter so that they are closer to the shape they will be in the final pastry.

Before rolling and folding the chilled dough, give it a few hearty whacks with your rolling pin to soften it slightly.

Feel free to chill your dough at any point if the butter starts to get too warm. But do give the butter a few minutes to warm up slightly after the dough comes out of the fridge between turns.

Tender Free-form Galette Dough

MAKES ENOUGH DOUGH FOR 1 GALETTE CRUST

This recipe uses the same ingredients as the Laminated Butter Pie Pastry (page 5), but it is made with a different method, for a completely different crust.

In a food processor, the dough becomes a more uniform mixture. Some of the fat will coat the proteins in the flour and keep it from developing gluten (as in a shortbread cookie), making for an extra-tender dough. The remaining butter pebbles will melt in the oven and create steam, again contributing to the overall tenderness.

This pastry is not exactly flaky the way a laminated dough is, and it isn't great for pies because it's too soft to cut and slice neatly under a heavy filling. Instead, I like this dough for free-form galettes, where the crust is in direct contact with the hot baking sheet, so it becomes brown and crisp.

1¼ cups (170 grams) all-purpose flour

1 tablespoon (13 grams) granulated sugar

½ teaspoon kosher salt

8 tablespoons (1 stick; 113 grams) cold butter, cut into pieces

¼ to ⅓ cup (60 to 75 grams) water

If you want to go the extra mile, use heavy cream instead of water, which will further inhibit gluten development.

To the bowl of a food processor, add the flour, sugar, and salt and pulse to combine. Add the butter and pulse until the mixture resembles coarse sand, with some larger pieces. Add ¼ cup water and pulse until the dough is evenly moistened and holds together when you squeeze a small clump with your fingers. If necessary, add more water a teaspoon at a time, pulsing, but stop before the dough becomes wet. Do not process the dough until it forms a ball; it should still be crumbly.

Tip the dough out onto a piece of plastic wrap and use the edges of the plastic to bring it together and then form it into a small, flat disk. Chill the dough for at least 1 hour before using. It can be stored, well wrapped, in the refrigerator for up to 3 days or frozen for up to 1 month. (Don't leave pastry dough in the fridge for too long, though, or it will turn gray. That means it's time for the compost bin.)

Rough Puff Pastry

MAKES ENOUGH DOUGH FOR 2 SINGLE PIECRUSTS

Traditional puff pastry is made by wrapping dough around a block of butter and laminating (rolling and folding) it to create layers. To make the technique easier, clever pastry chefs created "rough puff pastry," where the butter is simply cut into the flour mixture as for a pie dough and then laminated from there. The results are just as good and considerably easier to achieve. Use rough puff pastry to make my ultra-lux Chocolate Crémeux Slice (page 22), sugary palmiers, and crisp cheese straws.

This recipe uses more butter and more turns to create even more layers than the Laminated Butter Pie Pastry (page 5). Besides creating flakiness, the fat is also adding flavor, which is why I like to use salted butter. Cultured butter, which has been fermented, would also be lovely here. European butter, which has a bit more butterfat than most American butters, would also work well in this recipe, and it will make the dough a little easier to roll out.

2 cups (272 grams) all-purpose four

½ teaspoon kosher salt

18 tablespoons (2¼ sticks; 254 grams) cold butter, cut into very thin slices

6 to 8 tablespoons (90 to 120 grams) ice water

In a large bowl, combine the flour, salt, and butter. Add 6 tablespoons water and mix with a fork just until the dough comes together; if necessary, add up to 2 tablespoons more water a little at a time.

Turn the mixture out onto a floured work surface and roll it into a 12 x 10-inch rectangle, with a short side nearest you. Use a bench scraper to fold the dough into thirds, like a business letter: Fold the bottom third up over the center and then fold the top third down over that. The dough will be crumbly. Rotate the dough so that the folded edge is to the left. Roll, fold, and turn the dough two more times, lightly flouring the work surface as necessary. Wrap in plastic wrap and refrigerate for at least 30 minutes.

Repeat the rolling and folding step one more time (for a total of 6 turns), wrap, and refrigerate for at least 1 hour before using.

The dough can be stored, well wrapped, for up to 2 days in the refrigerator or 1 month in the freezer. Thaw frozen dough in the fridge before using.

The dough will start out insanely crumbly. Don't worry. Just keep going, and it will come together as the butter works into it. The bench scraper is your friend here.

Make sure the oven is properly preheated before baking puff pastry so that the water turns to steam quickly and lifts your dough to flaky perfection. If it isn't, the water will leach out and sog everything up.

Browned-Butter Shortbread

MAKES 12 COOKIES

For this shortbread dough, the butter coats the flour, thereby inhibiting gluten formation and making the pastry "short," or crumbly, when baked. The butter is melted so it coats the flour even more thoroughly. Browning the butter, or more specifically the milk solids in the butter, also adds a distinctive nutty flavor. Delicious on their own, these shortbread cookies would also be nice dipped in chocolate or sandwiched with jam.

16 tablespoons (2 sticks; 226 grams) butter, plus more for the pan

 2 cups (272 grams) all-purpose flour

 ½ cup (100 grams) granulated sugar, plus more for sprinkling

 ½ teaspoon kosher salt

 2 teaspoons pure vanilla extract

Preheat the oven to 350°F. Butter a 9-inch fluted tart pan with a removable bottom.

In a small bowl, combine the flour, sugar, and salt.

Put the butter in a medium light-colored saucepan and cook over medium-high heat, swirling the pan occasionally, until the butter has melted, the milk solids have turned golden brown, and the butter smells nutty, 6 to 8 minutes. Immediately remove the pan from the heat and pour the butter into a large heatproof bowl to cool slightly, 10 minutes or so.

Add the flour mixture and vanilla to the butter and stir to combine. Press the dough evenly over the bottom of the prepared pan and sprinkle with sugar.

Bake the shortbread until golden brown, 40 to 45 minutes.

Transfer to a rack and allow to cool for 15 minutes, then cut into 12 triangles while the shortbread is still warm. Let the shortbread cool completely, then remove from the pan, separating the wedges if necessary.

Store the cookies in an airtight container at room temperature for up to 1 week or in the freezer for 1 month.

When making browned butter, use a light-colored pan so that you can easily see the milk solids change color.

You can strain out the browned bits if you want, but they carry flavor. I prefer to leave them in. Easier and tastier!

Browned-Butter Blackberry Bars

MAKES 24 BARS

This is my version of a St. Louis Gooey Butter Cake, with a few tweaks. I wanted it to be more bar than cake and to have more to offer than just buttery sweetness. Browned butter and tangy blackberries give the bars a little more dimension. And I promise you, the smell as these bake will make everyone swoon.

BASE

- 8 tablespoons (1 stick; 113 grams) butter, at room temperature, plus more for the pan
- ½ cup (120 grams) whole milk, heated to 110° to 115°F
- 1½ teaspoons active dry yeast
- 1¾ cups (238 grams) all-purpose flour
- ¼ cup (50 grams) granulated sugar
- ½ teaspoon kosher salt
- 1 large (50 grams) egg, at room temperature
- 2 large (40 grams) egg yolks, at room temperature
- 1½ teaspoons pure vanilla extract

TOPPING

- 12 tablespoons (1½ sticks; 170 grams) butter
- 1¼ cups (225 grams) granulated sugar
- ¾ teaspoon kosher salt
- 1 large (50 grams) egg
- 1 cup (136 grams) all-purpose flour
- 3 tablespoons (63 grams) Lyle's Golden Syrup
- 2 tablespoons (30 grams) water
- 1 tablespoon (14 grams) pure vanilla extract
- 1 teaspoon finely grated lemon zest
- 12 ounces (340 grams) blackberries, halved if large

  Confectioners' sugar for sprinkling

Golden syrup is a honey-like syrup made from sugarcane. It has a lovely toasty sweetness and is worth seeking out. But corn syrup is a fine, slightly less-delicious substitute if you can't find it.

PREPARE THE BASE. Butter a 13 x 9-inch baking pan and line it with parchment paper, leaving a 2-inch overhang on the two long sides.

In the bowl of a stand mixer fitted with the dough hook, combine the milk and yeast. Let stand until the yeast is foamy, about 5 minutes. Add the flour, sugar, and salt to the yeast mixture and mix for a few minutes to combine. With the mixer running, add the egg and egg yolks and mix until combined, about 2 minutes. The dough will still look a little crumbly. Add the butter a little bit at a time, then beat until the dough is smooth and elastic.

continues

Tip the dough out into the prepared pan and use an offset spatula to spread it evenly over the bottom. It may seem thin, but make sure to get it all the way to the edges of the pan. Cover with plastic wrap and set aside to rise until nice and puffy. This will take a while, about 2 hours.

MEANWHILE, PREPARE THE TOPPING. In a medium light-colored saucepan, cook the butter over medium-high heat, swirling the pan occasionally, until it has melted, the milk solids have turned golden brown, and the butter smells nutty, about 8 minutes. Transfer the butter to a medium bowl, including all the browned bits, and pop it into the fridge to firm up.

Preheat the oven to 350°F.

When the dough has puffed, add the sugar and salt to the browned butter and beat with an electric mixer until fluffy, about 3 minutes. Add the egg and beat to combine. On low speed, beat in the flour, then beat in the golden syrup, water, vanilla, and lemon zest.

Dollop the batter evenly over the risen dough and then spread it into an even layer. (Work gently so as not to deflate the dough.) Scatter the blackberries over the top.

Bake until the topping is golden brown, 35 to 40 minutes. The center will still look slightly loose, but it will firm up as it cools. Transfer the pan to a rack to cool completely.

Use the parchment overhang to lift the bar out onto a cutting board. Sprinkle evenly with confectioners' sugar and cut into 24 equal pieces.

The bars can be stored in an airtight container at room temperature for up to 3 days.

Slightly damp fingertips work well here.

Gooey Cranberry Crumb Cake

SERVES 24

When I was developing this recipe, I was going for a crisp crumb topping like the golden crown atop the Banana Crumb Cake (page 152), but I used room-temperature butter instead of melted butter in my first test. Melting butter changes its fat structure completely and intead of the crisp crumbs I was expecting, the softened butter gave the topping a gooey caramel texture. It worked so nicely with the super-tart cranberries that I decided to embrace my mistake. I like the sweet-tart combo of cake and cranberries, but blueberries, raspberries, or blackberries would also be nice here.

CRUMB

- 6 tablespoons (¾ stick; 85 grams) butter, cut into pieces, at room temperature, plus more for the pan
- 1½ cups (300 grams) packed light brown sugar
- ¾ cup (102 grams) all-purpose flour
- ½ teaspoon kosher salt

CAKE

- 2½ cups (340 grams) all-purpose flour
- 1½ teaspoons baking powder
- ¾ teaspoon kosher salt
- ½ teaspoon baking soda
- 1¼ cups (250 grams) granulated sugar
- 8 tablespoons (1 stick; 113 grams) butter, at room temperature
- 1 tablespoon (6 grams) finely grated orange zest
- 2 large (100 grams) eggs, at room temperature
- 2 teaspoons pure vanilla extract
- 1 cup (160 grams) full-fat sour cream, at room temperature
- 3 cups (320 grams) fresh or frozen cranberries, not thawed if frozen

Frozen cranberries will immediately cool and stiffen the batter, but that's just fine, though the cake will take a few extra minutes to bake through.

Preheat the oven to 350°F. Butter a 13 x 9-inch baking pan and line it with parchment paper, leaving a 2-inch overhang on the two long sides. Butter the parchment.

PREPARE THE CRUMB. In a medium bowl, whisk together the brown sugar, flour, and salt. Add the butter and, with an electric mixer on medium speed, mix it in. The mixture should look like evenly moistened sand. Set aside.

PREPARE THE CAKE. In another medium bowl, whisk together the flour, baking powder, salt, and baking soda.

In a large bowl, beat the sugar, butter, and orange zest with the mixer on medium until light and fluffy, about 3 minutes. Add the eggs one at a time, mixing well and scraping down the bowl as necessary. Beat in the vanilla. Beat in half of the flour mixture, then the sour cream, and then the remaining flour mixture. Do not overmix.

Transfer half of the batter to the prepared pan and spread it evenly with an offset spatula. (The layer will be thin.) Sprinkle about 1 cup of the crumb mixture evenly over the top. Top with about half of the cranberries.

Dollop the remaining batter over the top of the cranberries and spread it out evenly with the offset spatula. Top with the remaining cranberries. Sprinkle the remaining crumb mixture evenly over the top, squeezing it into various-sized pieces.

Bake the cake until a toothpick inserted into the center comes out with a few moist crumbs attached. If you used fresh cranberries, start checking the cake at around 35 minutes. If the cranberries were frozen, the cake may take up to 55 minutes.

Transfer the pan to a rack and let cool completely.

Using the parchment overhang, carefully lift out the cake and transfer it to a cutting board to cut and serve.

The cake can be stored in an airtight container at room temperature for up to 5 days, or frozen for 1 month; thaw at room temperature before serving. (The sugary topping may become a bit moist over time, but the cake will still taste delicious.)

Beating the orange zest with the butter allows its flavor to permeate the batter more effectively.

Chocolate, Banana, and Oat Cookies

MAKES ABOUT 30 COOKIES

These are the perfect cookies for that almost-forgotten school bake sale. They come together quickly, don't require any special ingredients or equipment, and boast a soft and chewy texture and familiar flavors sure to please the masses.

10 tablespoons (1¼ sticks; 141 grams) butter, at room temperature

⅓ cup (67 grams) granulated sugar

½ cup (100 grams) packed light or dark brown sugar

1 large (50 grams) egg, at room temperature

½ cup (105 grams) mashed banana (from 1 overripe banana)

1½ teaspoons pure vanilla extract

1 cup (136 grams) all-purpose flour

1 teaspoon baking soda

½ teaspoon kosher salt

½ teaspoon ground cinnamon

2½ cups (200 grams) old-fashioned rolled oats

1¼ cups (175 grams) good-quality milk chocolate, chopped

To save overripe bananas, peel them and freeze in an airtight container. If you want to be very organized, you can freeze mashed bananas in 1-cup portions.

Milk chocolate really varies in quality. Search out the best—it's worth it.

Preheat the oven to 350°F, with the racks in the upper and lower thirds of the oven. Line two baking sheets with parchment paper.

In a large bowl, using a wooden spoon, beat the butter, granulated sugar, and brown sugar until creamy. Stir in the egg, banana mash, and vanilla.

In a small bowl, whisk together the flour, baking soda, salt, and cinnamon. Add to the butter mixture and stir to combine, scraping down the sides of the bowl as necessary. Stir in the oats and chocolate.

Drop the cookies in 2-tablespoon scoops, at least 2 inches apart, onto the prepared baking sheets. With the back of a spatula, flatten each scoop slightly.

Bake the cookies until golden brown and set, 8 to 11 minutes, rotating the sheets halfway through. Transfer the sheets to racks and let the cookies cool for a few minutes, then transfer the cookies to racks to cool completely. Repeat with the remaining dough.

The cookies can be stored in an airtight container at room temperature for up to 3 days or in the freezer for up to 1 month.

If you've frozen the banana mash, make sure to use all the liquid that will appear after thawing. That's banana goodness you don't want to throw away. Stir the liquid into the thawed mash before you measure out the amount you need.

Fried Blueberry Mini Pies

Cute and portable, these sweet-tart mini pies are the perfect dessert eaten out of hand on a warm summer evening.

Adding an egg white to the dough transforms it into a dessert hybrid—flaky like pastry, thanks to the lamination technique, but chewy like a doughnut. The white also makes the dough more forgiving when it comes to rolling.

Wild blueberries have a more concentrated flavor than cultivated berries, which lends itself nicely to baking. The fresh berries can be somewhat hard to find, even during their summer season, but frozen wild blueberries make a perfect year-round substitute. I keep a giant bag of them in the freezer at all times. (They also make an excellent dessert eaten out of hand. Just ask my kiddo.)

PASTRY

- 1½ cups (204 grams) all-purpose flour, plus more for rolling
- 2 teaspoons granulated sugar
- ½ teaspoon kosher salt
- 8 tablespoons (1 stick; 113 grams) butter, cut into pieces
- 1 large (30 grams) egg white
- 4 to 6 tablespoons (60 to 90 grams) cold water

FILLING

- 1½ cups (247 grams) fresh or frozen wild blueberries, not thawed if frozen
- 1 teaspoon fresh lemon juice
- 3 tablespoons (38 grams) granulated sugar
- 1 tablespoon (14 grams) butter
- 1 tablespoon (8 grams) cornstarch
- ½ vanilla bean, split lengthwise and seeds scraped out, seeds and bean reserved
- Pinch of kosher salt

Vegetable oil for deep-frying

Granulated sugar for tossing

PREPARE THE PASTRY. In a medium bowl, whisk together the flour, sugar, and salt. Add the butter and toss to combine. Smoosh each of the butter pieces flat.

In a small bowl, whisk together the egg white and 4 tablespoons water. Make a well in the center of the flour mixture, add the egg white mixture, and stir with a fork to combine. If the flour mixture is evenly moistened and you can press the crumbs together, you don't need any more water. If necessary, add up to 2 tablespoons more water a little bit at a time.

Tip the dough out, shape it into a disk, and wrap in plastic wrap. Refrigerate for at least 30 minutes.

On a lightly floured surface, roll the dough out into a large rectangle. Fold the top half of the dough over the bottom half. Then bring the left side over the right side. Repeat the rolling and folding process three more times.

Wrap the dough again and refrigerate for 30 minutes to an hour.

MEANWHILE, PREPARE THE FILLING. In a medium saucepan, combine the blueberries, lemon juice, sugar, butter, cornstarch, vanilla bean and seeds, and salt and bring to a simmer over medium-low heat. Cook until the some of the liquid has evaporated, the fruit is tender, and the mixture has thickened, about 5 minutes. Remove from the heat and let cool completely, then remove and discard the vanilla bean.

On a lightly floured surface, roll the dough out into a 13-inch square. Using a 4½-inch round cutter, cut out 8 rounds and set them aside. (You can discard the dough scraps or fry them up with the pies and toss them in cinnamon sugar for a snack.)

Place about 2 tablespoons of the filling in the center of each round. Fold each round in half to make a half-moon shape, pressing the edges together, and seal tightly with a fork or a pastry wheel. Transfer to a lightly floured plate and refrigerate the pies for 1 hour.

When ready to fry, heat about 2 inches of oil to 350°F in a heavy pot over medium-high heat. Cook the pies in batches of 3 to avoid crowding the pot, carefully adjusting the heat as necessary to maintain the oil temperature: Fry until golden brown, about 4 minutes. Use a slotted spoon to transfer the pies to a paper towel–lined plate to cool slightly, then toss in sugar to serve. Don't wait too long to toss the pies in the sugar—their warmth will help the sugar adhere.

These pies are best served warm the day they're made.

A deep-fry or candy thermometer is your friend here. This inexpensive tool will help you to monitor the temperature of the oil. When I'm frying, I often have to turn the flame up or down as necessary to maintain the correct temperature. Oil that isn't hot enough will result in greasy pies.

Masala Chai Shortbread with **Prunes** and **Tea Glaze**

MAKES ABOUT 30 COOKIES

Don't skip the prunes! They add a lovely flavor of caramelized fruit that sings in these buttery tea-flavored cookies.

16 tablespoons (2 sticks; 226 grams) butter, at room temperature

¾ cup (150 grams) granulated sugar

4 large (80 grams) egg yolks

2½ cups (340 grams) all-purpose flour

½ teaspoon baking powder

1½ teaspoons cardamom seeds, crushed

1½ teaspoons ground cinnamon

1½ teaspoons ground ginger

½ teaspoon kosher salt

½ teaspoon freshly ground black pepper

½ cup (100 grams) chopped prunes

TEA GLAZE

½ cup (120 grams) heavy cream

2 tablespoons (8 grams) loose-leaf black tea

1 cup (120 grams) confectioners' sugar, sifted

To chop moist prunes easily, rub a little oil on your knife before you start.

It's tempting to skip, but be sure to sift the confectioners' sugar. Lumpy glaze is a sad sight.

Preground cardamom never tastes as nice as the freshly ground stuff. Look for cardamom pods that are somewhat moist and green, not yellow, and crush them with a mortar and pestle to release the black seeds inside. Remove and discard the husks and process the seeds according to the recipe.

Preground cinnamon and ginger are just fine. Just make sure the spices smell fresh and delicious.

In a large bowl, with an electric mixer on medium speed, beat the butter and sugar until combined and fluffy, about 2 minutes. Add the egg yolks and beat until combined, scraping down the sides of the bowl as necessary. Beat in the flour, baking powder, cardamom, cinnamon, ginger, salt, and pepper. Using a wooden spoon, gently mix in the prunes.

Divide the dough in half. Place each half on a sheet of plastic wrap and shape into a 2-inch-thick cylinder. (Two smaller cylinders are easier to work with than one big one.) Freeze the cylinders until solid, 2 to 4 hours.

Preheat the oven to 350°F, with racks in the upper and lower thirds of the oven. Line two rimmed baking sheets with parchment paper.

Using a sharp knife, cut one frozen dough cylinder into ¼-inch slices and place the slices on a prepared sheet. Repeat with the remaining dough.

Bake until the cookies are set and light golden around the edges, about 15 minutes, rotating the sheets halfway through. Transfer the cookies to racks and let cool completely.

PREPARE THE TEA GLAZE. In a small saucepan, bring the cream to a simmer. Immediately remove the pan from the heat and add the tea. Let steep for 10 minutes.

Strain the cream through a sieve set over a bowl and discard the tea. (Be sure to press on the solids to extract all the cream.) Put the confectioners' sugar in a bowl, add the tea cream, and whisk to combine.

Drizzle the glaze over the baked cookies. Let stand at room temperature until the glaze has set, about 1 hour.

The cookies can be stored in an airtight container at room temperature for up to 1 week or frozen for up to 1 month. Thaw at room temperature before serving.

Toasted Coconut Oat Cookies

MAKES 24 COOKIES

These cookies are simple, chewy perfection. Salted butter gives them a welcome savory edge without being too salty.

- 1½ cups (204 grams) all-purpose flour
- 1 teaspoon baking soda
- 1 teaspoon kosher salt
- 12 tablespoons (1½ sticks; 170 grams) butter, at room temperature
- ½ cup (112 grams) coconut oil, softened slightly
- ¾ cup (150 grams) packed dark brown sugar
- ½ cup (100 grams) granulated sugar
- 1 large (50 grams) egg
- 2 teaspoons pure vanilla extract
- 2 cups (160 grams) old-fashioned rolled oats
- 1 cup (68 grams) toasted sweetened shredded coconut

To toast coconut, spread it in an even layer on a light-colored baking sheet and bake in a 350°F oven, stirring often, for 5 to 10 minutes. (A dark sheet will encourage burning.) You can also toast coconut in a dry skillet over medium heat, stirring often, but I find that the oven produces a more even browning.

In a medium bowl, whisk together the flour, baking soda, and salt. Set aside.

In a large bowl, with an electric mixer on medium speed, beat together the butter, coconut oil, brown sugar, and granulated sugar until very light, about 5 minutes. You don't want to see any little pieces of coconut oil. Add the egg and vanilla and beat until well combined, scraping down the sides of the bowl as necessary.

Add the flour mixture and beat on low just until combined. Add the oats and coconut and mix briefly to combine.

Tip the dough out, shape it into about an 8-inch square, and wrap in plastic wrap. Chill for at least 24 hours and up to 2 days. Freeze the dough for up to 1 month.

Preheat the oven to 375°F. Line three rimmed baking sheets with parchment paper. Let the dough stand at room temperature for a few minutes to soften slightly.

Cut the dough into 24 squares. Roll each one into a ball and set 8 cookies evenly spaced on one of the prepared sheets. Bake the cookies until set and golden brown, 12 to 14 minutes. Transfer the cookies to a rack to cool. Repeat with the remaining dough and the other prepared sheets. (I prefer to bake these cookies one sheet at a time for more consistent results.)

The cookies can be stored in an airtight container at room temperature for up to 1 week or frozen for up to 1 month. Thaw at room temperature before serving.

If you bake these without a rest in the fridge, they will spread out and become the perfect crisp cookies for ice cream sandwiches. I highly recommend this.

Chocolate Crémeux Slice

This is my version of a British custard slice, except it has crémeux between the pieces of puff pastry. Crémeux—its name means creamy in French—is a silky custard that lives somewhere between mousse and pudding. I want to live there too.

CHOCOLATE CRÉMEUX

- 1¾ cups (245 grams) bittersweet chocolate, finely chopped
- ¾ cup (180 grams) heavy cream
- ¾ cup (180 grams) whole milk
- 4 large (80 grams) egg yolks
- ¼ cup (50 grams) granulated sugar
- ¾ teaspoon kosher salt

PASTRY

- 1 recipe Rough Puff Pastry (page 7), cut into 2 pieces
- Granulated sugar for rolling
- Confectioners' sugar for dusting

If you're short on time, skip the puff pastry altogether and serve the crémeux topped with whipped cream.

PREPARE THE CHOCOLATE CRÉMEUX. Put the chocolate in a medium heatproof bowl and set aside.

In a small saucepan, whisk together the cream, milk, egg yolks, sugar, and salt and cook over medium heat, stirring constantly with a wooden spoon, until the custard has thickened slightly, about 6 minutes. Using a fingertip, you should be able to draw a clear line through the custard on the back of the spoon. Pour the custard through a fine-mesh sieve onto the chocolate and let stand for 1 minute.

Using an immersion blender, blend the custard with the chocolate until creamy and smooth, 1 to 2 minutes. (You could also do this in a regular blender.) Cover with plastic wrap pressed directly against the surface of the custard, and chill until set, at least 3 hours.

PREPARE THE PASTRY. Preheat the oven to 375°F. Line two rimmed baking sheets with parchment paper.

Lightly sprinkle a work surface with granulated sugar and roll out one piece of the pastry dough into about a 10-inch square. Trim the edges so you have a neat square and discard the excess dough. Repeat with the remaining dough. Wrap each square in plastic wrap and freeze for 10 to 15 minutes.

Transfer the squares to the lined baking sheets. If you have two wire racks that are at least 1 inch high, set these over the squares of dough; this will help them bake evenly. But if you don't have them, don't worry. The final result will be a little bit more rustic but just as tasty.

Bake until the pastry is puffed and deeply golden brown, about 30 minutes, rotating the sheets halfway through. Transfer to racks to cool completely.

To serve, set one sheet of pastry on a large serving plate. Transfer the chocolate crémeux to a pastry bag fitted with a fluted tip and pipe rosettes of crémeux over the top of the pastry. Top with the remaining sheet of pastry. Chill for 30 minutes or up to 3 hours. Dust lightly with confectioners' sugar. Use a serrated knife to cut it into slices and serve immediately.

This is best the day it's assembled.

Using a pastry bag to pipe rosettes of crémeux is not essential, but it does make it look pretty. First cut a small hole in the tip of the bag, if necessary, and add a fluted tip over it. If you have a coupler, use it to lock the tip into place. Then fold the tip over, set the bag in a large glass, and fold the edges of the bag over the rim of the glass. Fill the bag and twist the top to close.

Blackberry-Rye Cream Scones

MAKES 8 SCONES

Rye flour adds a pleasant nuttiness to these tender breakfast scones. And since you'll have some flour left over, I suggest you try the Raspberry Rye-Balsamic Tart on page 40 next.

- ¾ cup (180 grams) cold heavy cream, plus more for brushing
- 1 large (50 grams) egg
- 1½ teaspoons pure vanilla extract
- 1½ to 1¾ cups (204 to 238 grams) all-purpose flour
- ½ cup (51 grams) rye flour
- ⅓ cup (67 grams) granulated sugar
- 2 teaspoons baking powder
- 1 teaspoon freshly grated nutmeg (or ½ teaspoon ground)
- ½ teaspoon kosher salt
- 6 tablespoons (¾ stick; 85 grams) cold butter, cut into small pieces
- 6 ounces (165 grams) blackberries, chopped (about 1 cup)
- Sanding sugar for sprinkling (optional)

Turbinado sugar is a great substitute if you don't have sanding sugar. Even granulated sugar will give the exterior a pleasant sheen.

In a small bowl, mix together the cream, egg, and vanilla.

In a large bowl, whisk together the all-purpose flour, rye flour, granulated sugar, baking powder, nutmeg, and salt. Smoosh the butter into the flour mixture with your fingers. The goal is to make evenly dispersed butter flakes. Add the blackberries and gently toss until just combined.

Drizzle in the cream mixture and stir with a fork until combined. Try not to smash the blackberries. Don't overmix this dough; it's OK if there is a tiny bit of dry mixture at the bottom of the bowl. For scones, it's better to slightly undermix rather than overmix the dough.

Tip the dough out onto a piece of parchment paper and pat it into a 6-inch circle. Using a sharp knife or a bench scraper, cut the circle into 8 equal triangles, but leave the round intact for the moment. Transfer the dough, still on the parchment, to a plate and freeze for at least 15 minutes to firm up. (You can freeze the unbaked scones for another day. Bake them from frozen, brushing them with the cream and sprinkling with sanding sugar, if using, just before baking. Increase the baking time by a minute or two.)

Preheat the oven to 375°F.

Transfer the scones, still on the paper, to a rimmed baking sheet. Space the scones out evenly and brush the tops with heavy cream. Sprinkle with sanding sugar, if desired.

Bake until the scones are golden brown and set, about 22 minutes. A toothpick inserted into the center of one scone should come out clean. Transfer the sheet to a rack to cool slightly.

Serve warm or at room temperature. The scones are best the day they're made.

If at any point the butter starts to melt into the dough as you prepare it, pop the dough into the fridge for a quick chill before moving forward.

Buckwheat Walnut Linzer Cookies

Jam is a nice filling for these sandwiched butter cookies, but melted chocolate, almond butter, or Biscoff spread would be lovely too!

1 cup (120 grams) walnuts

1 cup (200 grams) granulated sugar

24 tablespoons (3 sticks; 339 grams) butter, softened

1½ teaspoons ground cinnamon

1 teaspoon kosher salt

2 large (40 grams) egg yolks

1½ teaspoons pure vanilla extract

2 cups (272 grams) all-purpose flour, plus more for rolling

2 cups (280 grams) buckwheat flour

Confectioners' sugar for dusting

About ¾ cup (195 grams) of your favorite jam for filling

The butter should be slightly softer than room-temperature butter. The goal is for it to be fully incorporated into the dough for crisp "short" cookies. If you're softening butter in the microwave as I suggest on page 3, add another 6 to 8 seconds.

In the bowl of a food processor, combine the walnuts and sugar and process until the nuts are finely ground. Add the butter, cinnamon, and salt and process until well combined. Add the egg yolks and vanilla extract and process until smooth. Add the flours and pulse until a shaggy dough forms.

Tip the dough out, divide it in half, and place each half on a piece of plastic wrap. Form the dough into two rectangles, then wrap and refrigerate until firm, at least 1 hour. (You can freeze this dough, well wrapped, for up to 3 months.)

Preheat the oven to 350°F. Line two rimmed baking sheets with parchment paper.

On a lightly floured surface, roll one portion of dough out into a 13 x 11-inch rectangle about ⅛ inch thick. Use a fluted pastry wheel to trim ½ inch from each side, then cut the dough into 2-inch squares. (If your dough gets too soft, transfer it to a baking sheet and pop it into the fridge to chill.) Transfer the squares to one of the prepared baking sheets, about 1 inch apart. Use a ¼-inch cutter (hearts are always nice!) to make a cutout in the center of half of the squares. You can bake the cutouts separately if you'd like. They'll bake faster than the squares.

Bake the cookies until set and golden brown around the edges, 10 to 13 minutes. Let cool on the sheet on a rack for 5 minutes, then transfer them to another rack to cool completely. Meanwhile, repeat with the remaining rectangle of dough, and use the second prepared baking sheet. (You can freeze these guys unfilled for up to 3 months. They will thaw at room temperature as you fill them.)

Transfer all the cookies with cut-out centers to a tray and dust them with confectioners' sugar. Flip the remaining cookies over and spread some jam on each one, then top with one of the dusted cookies. Store in an airtight container at room temperature for up to 3 days.

Square cookies, as opposed to round ones, leave less waste when you cut them out.

Date and Almond Butter Crescent Cookies

MAKES 48 COOKIES

Did you know that you can swap in cottage cheese for yogurt, sour cream, or buttermilk in your favorite cakes and pancakes? Its acidity works with the leavener in the recipe to create loft and its fat creates a moist crumb. For these flaky rolled cookies, I work cottage cheese along with butter into the dough to make a super-tender and pliable pastry.

DOUGH

- 16 tablespoons (2 sticks; 226 grams) butter, at room temperature
- 1 cup (225 grams) full-fat cottage cheese, at room temperature
- 2 cups (272 grams) all-purpose flour, plus more for rolling
- ½ teaspoon kosher salt

FILLING

- 6 ounces (175 grams) pitted dates (about 10), chopped
- ¼ cup (64 grams) almond butter
- 2 tablespoons (25 grams) light or dark brown sugar
- 2 tablespoons (39 grams) maple syrup
- ½ teaspoon ground cinnamon
- Pinch of kosher salt

TO FINISH

- 1 large (50 grams) egg, beaten
- Sanding sugar for sprinkling

Look for cottage cheese without added gums and stabilizers.

Don't waste money on fancy Medjool dates for this recipe. And don't skip the soaking step. It's important to reintroduce enough moisture into the dried fruit to ensure it doesn't rob moisture from the cookie itself. That goes for other recipes too!

PREPARE THE DOUGH. In a large bowl, with an electric mixer on medium speed, beat the butter and cottage cheese together until well combined, about 2 minutes. Add the flour and salt and beat just until combined.

Tip the dough out and divide it into 4 equal portions. (You will still be able to see some cottage cheese curds; that's OK!) Wrap each portion in plastic wrap and flatten into a disk. Chill the dough for at least 2 hours, and up to 2 days.

PREPARE THE FILLING. Put the dates in a small bowl, pour enough boiling water over them to cover completely, and let them soak at room temperature for 10 minutes.

Remove the dates from the water and transfer to a food processor. Add the almond butter, brown sugar, maple syrup, cinnamon, and salt and process until smooth.

Preheat the oven to 350°F, with racks in the upper and lower thirds of the oven. Line two rimmed baking sheets with parchment paper.

On a floured surface, roll one disk of dough out into a 9½-inch circle. Use a 9-inch plate to trim the dough to a perfect circle. Spread one quarter of the filling over the dough.

Cut it into 12 equal triangles. Starting from the outer edge of each triangle, roll the cookies up into crescents. Carefully transfer them to one of the prepared baking sheets. Repeat with a second disk of dough and use the second baking sheet. (If at any point your dough gets too warm, transfer it to a baking sheet and pop it into the fridge for a few minutes.)

Carefully brush each crescent with the beaten egg and sprinkle with sanding sugar. Bake the cookies for 18 to 22 minutes, or until they are set and golden brown, rotating the sheets halfway through. Transfer the pans to racks to cool completely. Once the baking sheets are cool, transfer the cookies to a separate rack and repeat the process with the remaining dough.

Store cookies in an airtight container at room temperature for up to 1 week or frozen for up to 1 month.

Guava Bars

MAKES 27 BARS

Almost nothing smells better than a guava ripening on a kitchen counter. It reminds me of flowers, berries, honey, and goodness all wrapped up in one. Guava paste is a bit easier to find in the supermarket than the fruit, and it is equally tasty and plays very nicely with butter—especially in these soft bar cookies that teeter on the edge between shortbread and blondie.

16 tablespoons (2 sticks; 226 grams) butter, softened, plus more for the pan

¾ cup (150 grams) guava paste cut into small pieces

¼ cup (50 grams) granulated sugar

2¼ cups (306 grams) all-purpose flour

1 teaspoon kosher salt

Sanding sugar for sprinkling

Super-soft butter will help create a lovely short-crumbed cookie by inhibiting the formation of gluten.

Preheat the oven to 350°F. Butter a 9-inch square baking pan and line it with parchment paper, leaving a 2-inch overhang on two opposite sides.

In the bowl of a food processor, combine the guava paste and sugar and process to blend. Add the butter and process until smooth. Add the flour and salt and pulse to combine.

Tip the dough out into the prepared pan. Use a flat-bottomed measuring cup or an offset spatula to spread the dough out evenly and flatten it. Sprinkle sanding sugar generously over the top.

Bake until the dough is set, dry, and golden around the edges, 25 to 28 minutes. Transfer the pan to a rack and let cool slightly, about 15 minutes.

While the bar is still slightly warm, use the parchment overhang to transfer it to a cutting board. Cut into 27 small 1 by 3-inch rectangles. Let cool completely.

The cookies can be stored in an airtight container at room temperature for up to 1 week or frozen for up to 1 month. Thaw at room temperature before serving.

Combining the guava paste with the fat, in this case, butter, helps distribute and intensify the flavor.

Plum and Rose Pie Bars with Almonds

MAKES 24 BARS

Pretty, pink, and perfect for picnics, these fruit and crumb bars taste just as good as they look. Rose water can be overpowering, but the tart floral flavor of the plums balances it nicely.

CRUST

- 14 tablespoons (1¾ sticks; 198 grams) cold butter, cut into pieces, plus more for the pan
- ¾ cup (75 grams) sliced almonds
- ½ cup (100 grams) packed light or dark brown sugar
- 2½ cups (340 grams) all-purpose flour
- 1½ teaspoons baking powder
- ¾ teaspoon kosher salt
- 1 large (50 grams) egg

JAM

- 5 to 6 small red plums, pitted and chopped (675 grams)
- ½ cup (100 grams) granulated sugar
- 1 tablespoon (8 grams) cornstarch
- 1½ teaspoons fresh lemon juice
- 2 teaspoons rose water

↳ Look for rose water that comes in a dark bottle. As with vanilla extract, heat and sunlight can damage its delicate flavor.

Preheat the oven to 350°F. Butter an 8- or 9-inch square baking pan and line it with parchment paper, leaving a 2-inch overhang on two opposite sides.

PREPARE THE CRUST. In the bowl of a food processor, combine the almonds and brown sugar and process until the almonds are finely ground. Add the flour, baking powder, and salt and pulse to combine. Add the butter and pulse to combine, then pulse in the egg. The dough will be crumbly.

Transfer about two thirds of the dough mixture to the prepared pan. Spread it out into an even layer and flatten it with an offset spatula or a flat-bottomed measuring cup. (Chill the remaining dough until ready to use.)

Bake the crust until it is golden brown, 24 to 26 minutes.

MEANWHILE, PREPARE THE JAM. In a medium saucepan, combine the plums, sugar, and cornstarch and cook over medium heat, stirring occasionally, until the mixture is bubbling and the fruit has broken down and thickened, 10 to 15 minutes.

Remove the jam from the heat and stir in the lemon juice and rose water. Let cool slightly. (You should have about 1½ cups jam.) Top the baked bottom crust with the jam and spread it evenly. Scatter the remaining crumb mixture over the jam, squeezing it to make some larger clumps.

Bake until the top is golden brown, 28 to 32 minutes. Transfer the pan to a rack to cool completely.

Using the parchment overhang, transfer the bar to a cutting board and cut into squares to serve. The bars can be stored in an airtight container in the fridge for up to 3 days.

↳ I use metal binder clips to keep the parchment overhang in place.

Membrillo and Apple Hand Pies

I always have a block of membrillo, or quince paste, in my fridge. I often just snack on sticky slices, but little pieces of the paste also make a perfect lazy filling for hand pies wrapped in flaky butter pastry. I like the tartness of green apples against the sweet quince and the cheese but stone fruit, berries, or pears would be equally nice here.

Flour for rolling

1 recipe Laminated Butter Pie Pastry (page 5)

FILLING

1 cup (227 grams) mascarpone

2 teaspoons finely grated lemon zest

TO FINISH

1 large (50 grams) egg, lightly beaten

4½ ounces (127 grams) membrillo, mashed slightly to soften

1 tart Granny Smith apple, peeled, cored, and thinly sliced

GLAZE

1 cup (120 grams) confectioners' sugar, sifted

1 to 2 tablespoons (15 to 30 grams) whole milk, or more if needed

½ teaspoon pure vanilla extract

On a lightly floured surface, roll the dough out to a 14-inch square. Trim about ⅛ inch of dough from each edge and discard. Cut the dough into 9 equal squares. Transfer the squares to a parchment-lined rimmed baking sheet and freeze for at least 10 minutes.

PREPARE THE FILLING. In a small bowl, mix together the mascarpone and lemon zest.

Brush a 1-inch border of beaten egg on all four edges of each square. Spread some of the softened membrillo over the pastry. Set a few slices of apple near one corner of each square and top with about 2 tablespoons of the mascarpone mixture. Fold the unfilled side over the filled side of each square into a triangle and press tightly with a fork to seal the edges. For a more refined look, trim the edges of each pie with a pastry wheel; not only will this look nice, it will create a tighter seal.

Transfer the pies to a plate and place in the freezer for 15 minutes.

Preheat the oven to 400°F. Brush the pies with the remaining beaten egg. Cut a small X in the center of each pie to allow steam to escape. Bake the pies on the parchment-lined baking sheet until deep golden brown and puffed, 20 to 25 minutes, rotating the pan halfway through. Transfer the sheet to a rack to cool slightly.

MEANWHILE, PREPARE THE GLAZE. In a small bowl, whisk together the confectioners' sugar, milk, and vanilla. Add a bit more milk if necessary to make a loose glaze that will spread evenly.

Brush some of the glaze over each pie. Serve warm or at room temperature.

These are best served warm on the day they're made.

Hand pies leak sometimes. Mine occasionally do. Yours may too. It's OK. That's what the parchment paper is there for.

Freezing the pies briefly before baking helps keep the butter in the dough, where you want it, instead of oozing out.

Strawberry and Cream Corn Cake

Sweet corn shouldn't be reserved only for savory preparations. With juicy strawberries, fresh corn makes a cake that screams summer.

Be sure to cream the butter and sugar well before adding the wet ingredients. (See page 4 for a refresher on creaming butter and sugar.) Those little air bubbles are essential for creating a light and fluffy corn cake.

STRAWBERRY COMPOTE

- 1½ cups (300 grams) fresh or frozen strawberries
- ¼ cup (50 grams) granulated sugar
- 2 teaspoons cornstarch

WHIPPED CREAM

- ¼ cup (32 grams) confectioners' sugar
- 2 teaspoons cornstarch
- 2½ cups (600 grams) heavy cream

CAKE

- 1½ cups (175 grams) corn kernels, fresh or frozen
- 9 tablespoons (1⅛ stick; 127 grams) butter, at room temperature, plus more for the pan
- 2¼ cups (306 grams) all-purpose flour, plus more for the pan
- 1 tablespoon (12 grams) baking powder
- ¾ teaspoon kosher salt
- 6 tablespoons (90 grams) whole milk
- 1 tablespoon (14 grams) pure vanilla extract
- 1 cup plus 2 tablespoons (225 grams) sugar
- 5 large (100 grams) egg yolks, at room temperature

Swap in any seasonal fruit you like for the strawberries. Apples or pears would be unexpected but equally lovely. Increase the cornstarch by 1 teaspoon if the fruit is extra-juicy.

Cornstarch makes the whipped cream more stable. This is essential when whipped cream serves as a filling between layers of cake.

I don't use nonstick cake pans. Their dark surface encourages too much browning on the edges of tender cakes.

PREPARE THE STRAWBERRY COMPOTE. In a small saucepan, combine the strawberries and sugar and cook over medium heat, stirring occasionally and breaking the strawberries down with a wooden spoon or potato masher until the fruit has released its juices, about 6 minutes.

Transfer about 2 tablespoons of the strawberry juices to a small cup and whisk in the cornstarch. Add to the remaining strawberry mixture, bring to a boil, and cook, stirring, for about 2 minutes. Transfer to a bowl and let cool completely. (You should have about 1¼ cups jam.)

PREPARE THE WHIPPED CREAM. In a small saucepan, whisk together the confectioners' sugar, cornstarch, and ½ cup of the heavy cream. Bring to a low boil over medium heat and cook, stirring, until thickened to the consistency of thin pudding, reducing the heat as necessary to prevent scorching, about 2 minutes. Transfer the cream mixture to a large bowl and refrigerate until completely cold.

PREPARE THE CAKE. Preheat the oven to 350°F. Butter and flour an 8 x 2-inch round cake pan. Process the corn kernels in a blender or food processor until pureed. A little texture is OK. You should have ¾ cup puree.

In a small bowl, whisk together the flour, baking powder, and salt. In a medium bowl, whisk together the corn puree, milk, and vanilla extract. Set aside.

In a large bowl, with an electric mixer on medium speed, beat the butter and sugar together until light and fluffy, about 3 minutes. Add the egg yolks one at a time, beating well after each addition. Add half of the dry ingredients and beat to combine. Tip in the

continues

corn puree mixture and beat to combine. Add the remaining dry ingredients and beat just until incorporated.

Transfer the batter to the prepared pan and spread it evenly. Bake until the cake is set and golden around the edges, 40 to 50 minutes. A toothpick inserted into the center should come out with a few moist crumbs attached.

Transfer the pan to a rack to cool for 20 minutes, then flip the cake out onto the rack to cool completely.

ASSEMBLE THE CAKE. Whisk the cream/cornstarch mixture to loosen it, then add the remaining 2 cups heavy cream. Using an electric mixer on medium speed, beat the mixture until you have medium-stiff peaks, about 2 minutes.

Split the cake horizontally into thirds using a serrated knife. (Don't worry if the layers aren't perfect. We're going for a casual strawberry shortcake effect here.) Set the bottom cake layer, cut side up, on a serving plate and spread one third of the whipped cream over the top, then add one third of the strawberry jam and swirl the jam and cream together a bit. Top with another cake layer and another one third each of the cream and jam. Finish with the last cake layer, cut side down, and top with the remaining cream and compote.

Store in the fridge until ready to serve, but let the layers come to room temperature before serving. This cake is best the day it's assembled.

Apple Galette with Buckwheat and Honeycomb

SERVES 8 TO 10

Buckwheat flour, made from buckwheat groats, is nutty and pleasantly bitter. It can be overpowering, though, so I like to balance it with plenty of all-purpose flour. Buckwheat flour also happens to be gluten-free, so the all-purpose flour is essential to create structure in the dough. If buckwheat isn't your thing, you can swap in the Tender Free-form Tart Dough (page 6) for the buckwheat pastry.

Until very recently, I didn't know that you could eat honeycomb. You can, and you should! I like the crisp edges the best. The honeycomb sets off the tart apples and earthy buckwheat crust with a welcome sweetness. It looks lovely too.

PASTRY

- 1¼ cups (170 grams) all-purpose flour, plus more for the parchment
- ½ cup (69 grams) grams buckwheat flour
- 2 tablespoons (25 grams) granulated sugar
- ¾ teaspoon kosher salt
- 10 tablespoons (1¼ sticks; 141 grams) cold butter, cut into pieces
- 4 to 6 tablespoons (60 to 90 grams) ice water

FILLING

- 3 large crisp, tart apples, such as Pink Lady or Granny Smith, cored, and very thinly sliced (600 grams)
- ⅓ cup (67 grams) packed light brown sugar
- 1 tablespoon (8 grams) cornstarch
- 1 teaspoon finely grated lemon zest
- 2 teaspoons fresh lemon juice

- 1½ teaspoons ground cinnamon

TO FINISH

- 1 large (50 grams) egg, lightly beaten, for brushing
- Sanding sugar for sprinkling (optional)
- 2 tablespoons (¼ stick; 28 grams) butter, cut into small pieces

TO SERVE

- Honeycomb, broken into pieces
- Buckwheat groats, toasted
- Whipped cream

You can make buckwheat flour by blending buckwheat groats in a high-speed blender until finely ground. Leftover buckwheat flour? Try the Buckwheat Walnut Linzer Cookies on page 26.

For pretty slices and minimal work, slice each apple from top to bottom squarely around the core to remove the flesh in four chunks. Then cut each one into thin slices.

Because it's made in the food processor, this pastry will be delightfully tender. When fat coats some of the proteins in flour, gluten formation is limited.

PREPARE THE PASTRY. In the bowl of a food processor, combine the all-purpose flour, buckwheat flour, sugar, and salt and pulse to blend. Add the butter and pulse until the mixture resembles coarse sand, with some larger pieces. Add 4 tablespoons water and pulse until the dough is evenly moistened and holds together when you squeeze a clump in your fingers. If necessary, add up to 2 tablespoons more water a teaspoon at a time, and pulse again, but stop before the dough becomes too wet.

Tip the dough out onto a piece of plastic wrap and use the edges of the plastic to bring it together. Form it into a disk, wrap it well, and refrigerate for at least 1 hour or up to 2 days. Freeze for up to 1 month.

PREPARE THE FILLING. In a large bowl, toss together the apples, brown sugar, cornstarch, lemon zest, lemon juice, and cinnamon, being careful not to break the apple slices.

Roll the dough out ⅛ to ¼ inch thick on a piece of lightly floured parchment paper. Any shape is fine. Arrange the apples and any accumulated juice in the center, leaving at least a 1½-inch border all around. Fold the edges of the dough up over the edges of the

apples. Slide the galette, still on the paper, onto a baking sheet and freeze for 10 minutes.

Preheat the oven to 400°F.

Transfer the galette, still on the paper, to a rimmed baking sheet. Brush the edges of the pastry with the beaten egg and sprinkle with sanding sugar, if using. Top the apples with the cold butter pieces.

Bake the galette until the crust is golden brown, the apples are tender, and the juices are bubbling, about 40 minutes. Transfer to a rack to cool slightly.

Serve the galette warm or at room temperature, topped with pieces of honeycomb and toasted buckwheat groats, with whipped cream alongside. The galette is best the day it's made.

Raspberry-Rye-Balsamic Tart

SERVES 10

Rye flour has a malty, nutty flavor that brings out the richness of the balsamic vinegar in this jammy fruit tart. The recipe calls for only 4 teaspoons of vinegar, so use a good-quality, thicker one to get the most bang for your buck. This pastry is laminated, like puff pastry, for extra flakiness. The layering process is also important to strengthen the gluten for extra structure in the dough.

PASTRY

- 1½ cups (204 grams) all-purpose flour, plus more for rolling
- 1 cup (108 grams) rye flour
- 2 tablespoons (25 grams) granulated sugar
- 1 teaspoon kosher salt
- 16 tablespoons (2 sticks; 226 grams) cold butter, cut into thin slices
- ½ to ¾ cup (120 to 180 grams) ice water

FILLING

- 18 ounces (523 grams) fresh raspberries (4¼ cups)
- ½ cup (100 grams) packed light or dark brown sugar
- 2 tablespoons (16 grams) cornstarch
- 4 teaspoons (20 grams) aged balsamic vinegar
- 1 tablespoon (14 grams) pure vanilla extract
- 1 teaspoon finely grated lemon zest
- Pinch of kosher salt

TO FINISH

- 1 large (50 grams) egg, lightly beaten
- Sanding sugar for sprinkling

Don't use frozen raspberries here! They will sog out the crust.

Bubbling filling indicates that the cornstarch has had enough time to work its magic and thicken the filling.

This recipe would also work with an 8 x 12-inch tart pan.

PREPARE THE PASTRY. In a large bowl, whisk together the all-purpose flour, rye flour, sugar, and salt. Add the butter and toss to combine, then add ½ cup water and toss to combine. If everything is evenly moistened and you can press the crumbs together, you don't need to add any more water. If necessary, add up to another ¼ cup water a little bit at a time.

Tip the dough out onto a lightly floured work surface and using a floured pin roll it out to a ¼-inch-thick rectangle with the short sides on the top and bottom. Fold the top third of the dough down over the center and then fold the bottom third up over it (like folding a letter!). Repeat this rolling and folding process one more time.

Divide the dough in half, form it into two disks, and wrap in plastic wrap. Refrigerate the dough for at least 1 hour. (You can refrigerate it for up to 3 days or freeze it for up to 1 month.)

On a lightly floured surface, roll one disk of dough out to about a 10-inch circle. Transfer to a 9-inch fluted tart pan with a removable bottom. To transfer the pastry easily from your work surface to the tart pan, fold it in half and then into quarters. Set the folded pastry in the pan and unfold. It's a bit delicate, but if it tears or breaks, just press it back together. Ease the dough into the edges of the pan and then run a rolling pin over the top to trim the excess dough.

Freeze the tart shell for 15 minutes.

Preheat the oven to 425°F.

PREPARE THE FILLING. In a large bowl, toss together the raspberries, brown sugar, cornstarch, vinegar, vanilla, lemon zest, and salt. Add the raspberry mixture to the chilled tart shell and spread it out evenly.

Roll the other disk of dough out to a ¼-inch thickness. Using small cookie cutters of various sizes, cut decorative shapes out of the dough. Cover the top of the tart with the cutouts, then brush them with the beaten egg and sprinkle with sanding sugar. (You could also roll the second disk into a circle and then cut strips to make a lattice top.)

Set the tart on a rimmed baking sheet and bake for 30 to 40 minutes. If the filling isn't bubbling, continue baking until it is. If the pastry is browning too

much before the filling is cooked, you can tent the tart with foil.

Transfer the tart to a rack to cool completely, then remove the rim of the pan to serve. This tart is best the day it's made.

Canned-Apricot-Pistachio Galette

SERVES 8 TO 10

Perfectly ripe, fragrant apricots are elusive. The fruit I find is often mealy and flavorless. Canned apricots, on the other hand, are always tender and sweet. Added bonus: the syrup is delicious over yogurt and fruit, used as a sweetener for smoothies, or stirred into cocktails.

FILLING

- 2 cans (15.25 ounces each) apricots in syrup, drained, 2 tablespoons (60 grams) of the syrup reserved
- 6 tablespoons (75 grams) granulated sugar
- 1 tablespoon (8 grams) cornstarch
- 1 teaspoon finely grated lemon zest
- ½ cup (50 grams) chopped raw pistachios
- 1 large (50 grams) egg
- 4 tablespoons (½ stick; 57 grams) butter, at room temperature
- Pinch of kosher salt

PASTRY

- Flour for rolling
- 1 recipe Tender Free-form Galette Dough (page 6)

TO FINISH

- 1 large (50 grams) egg, lightly beaten
- Sanding sugar for sprinkling (optional)

When fruit is canned, it is set in a syrup that has a greater concentration of sugar than the fruit itself. Eventually that sugar syrup works its way into the fruit, cooking it in a way, softening the cell walls, and improving the overall flavor.

For the best flavor, use pistachios that are neither roasted nor salted.

Preheat the oven to 400°F.

PREPARE THE FILLING. Carefully arrange the apricots on a rimmed baking sheet or a plate; they will be soft and delicate.

In a small bowl, toss together 2 tablespoons of the sugar, the cornstarch, and lemon zest. Sprinkle over the apricots.

In the bowl of a food processor, combine the pistachios, reserved apricot syrup, the egg, 2 tablespoons of the butter, the salt, and the remaining ¼ cup sugar and process until a smooth paste forms.

PREPARE THE PASTRY. On a lightly floured piece of parchment, with a floured pin, roll the dough out into a 12-inch circle.

Spread the pistachio paste over the dough, leaving a 1½-inch border all around. Arrange the apricots on the dough. Lift the edges of the dough up over the fruit, folding and pleating the dough as necessary. Using the parchment paper, transfer the galette to a rimmed baking sheet. Freeze for 10 minutes.

Brush the pastry rim with the beaten egg and sprinkle with sanding sugar, if using. Dot the fruit with the remaining 2 tablespoons butter.

Bake the galette until the crust is deep golden brown, about 45 minutes. Some of the juices may leak out, but that's OK. Serve warm or at room temperature.

This galette is best the day it's made.

Thin and Crisp Chocolate Chippers

MAKES ABOUT 36 COOKIES

What do you get when you cross a chocolate chip cookie with a thin, delicate shortbread? A delightful cookie that tastes like the chipper you remember with an addictive new crunch.

This dough is made in the food processor with cold butter in order to prevent gluten development and limit loft, which makes the cookies both tender and crisp. The food processor also cuts the chocolate and walnuts down to the perfect size for rolling out the dough evenly for perfect cookies.

1 cup (136 grams) all-purpose flour, plus more for rolling

½ teaspoon baking soda

¾ teaspoon kosher salt

¼ cup (50 grams) granulated sugar

⅓ cup (67 grams) packed dark brown sugar

1 cup (140 grams) bittersweet chocolate, chopped

1¼ cups (114 grams) walnut halves

8 tablespoons (1 stick; 113 grams) cold butter, cut into pieces

1 large (30 grams) egg white

2 teaspoons pure vanilla extract

In the bowl of a food processor, combine the flour, baking soda, salt, granulated sugar, and brown sugar and pulse until well mixed. Add the chocolate, walnuts, and butter and process until the mixture resembles pebbly sand and the chocolate, walnuts, and butter are in small pieces and evenly dispersed.

Add the egg white and vanilla and pulse until the dough is evenly moistened. Tip the dough out and divide between two pieces of plastic wrap. Use the edges of the plastic to form the dough into two neat squares. Wrap them well and chill for at least 1 hour, and up to 3 days.

Preheat the oven to 350°F. Line two rimmed baking sheets with parchment paper.

Working with one square at a time, sandwich the dough between two pieces of lightly floured parchment and roll it to a scant ¼-inch thickness. Cut the dough into 1 x 2½-inch rectangles. Transfer the cookies to another baking sheet and freeze for 15 minutes. Repeat with the remaining dough.

Transfer the frozen cookies to the prepared sheets about 1 inch apart and bake until the cookies are set and golden brown, about 12 minutes. Transfer the baking sheets to racks to cool. The cookies will be fragile while they're still warm.

The cookies can be stored in an airtight container at room temperature for up to 1 week or frozen for up to 1 month. Thaw at room temperature before serving.

Resist the urge to make these cookies any thicker than ¼ inch. Thick cookies will bake up chewy instead of crisp.

A pizza or pastry wheel makes easy work of cutting the dough. If you want perfect rectangles, cut the dough into rectangles but do not separate the cookies. Bake the whole sheet and go over the cuts while the cookies are still warm, then separate them when cooled completely.

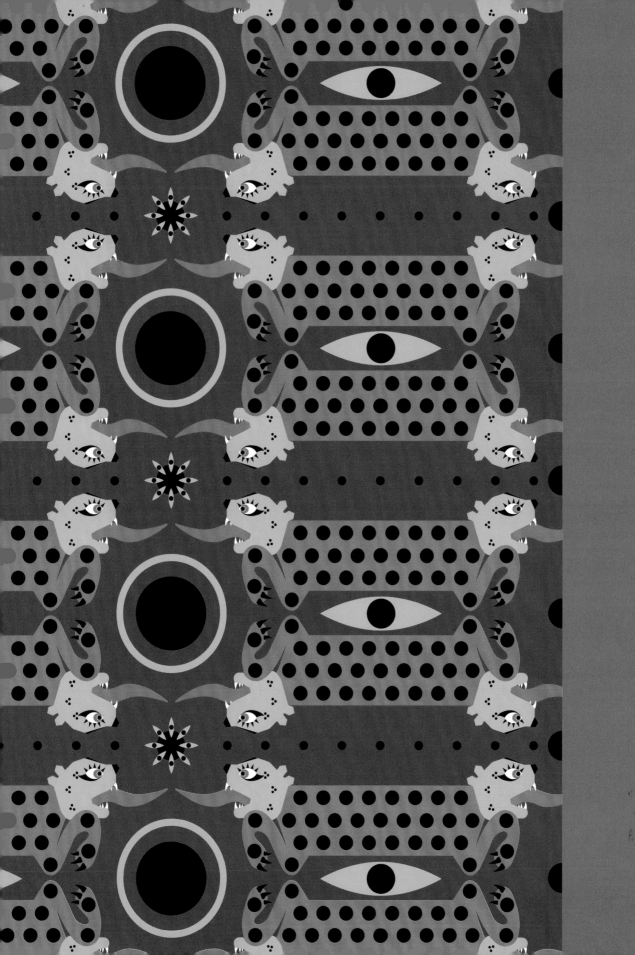

Sugar

Sweet teeth run in my family. When I was a kid, my dad taught me to sprinkle sugar over juicy summer cantaloupe, a completely unnecessary but truly delightful enhancement. We used sugar like salt—to bring out the already fabulous flavor of the fruit. Our dentist was less than impressed with the lesson I was learning, but I'm forever grateful to my dad and his proclivity for sugary treats.

When it comes to baking, sugar does so much more than add sweetness. Consider a soft cinnamon bun versus chewy pizza dough. The sugar in the dough inhibits gluten development, feeds the yeast, helps the buns retain moisture, and keeps them soft. Caramelized sugar creates those satisfying crisp browned edges on the perfect chocolate chip cookie. And when creamed with the butter, sugar helps give a cake its signature loft and texture.

The recipes in this chapter highlight the glory of sugar, illustrate how to use different types of sugar for different results, and demonstrate some of the best practices for simple candy making.

Think easy caramel sauce (page 52), crisp, melt-in-your-mouth meringues (page 60), hot-sugar-crust peach cake (page 66), and tender pumpkin cake (page 78).

I use four types of sugar for most of my baking:

GRANULATED SUGAR: To make this, the juice from sugarcane or sugar beets is processed into crystals.

BROWN SUGAR: Brown sugar is either semi-refined white sugar, where the natural molasses is still present, or white sugar with some molasses added back in. Dark brown sugar has more molasses than light brown sugar. I use them almost interchangeably, depending on how prominent I want that molasses flavor to be.

CONFECTIONERS' SUGAR: This is granulated sugar that's been pulverized into a powder and mixed with a little cornstarch to keep it from caking. You can make your own confectioners' sugar by processing 1 cup granulated sugar with 1 tablespoon cornstarch in a high-speed blender until powdery.

SANDING SUGAR: Also known as sparkling sugar, sanding sugar looks like granulated sugar with extra-large grains that won't melt or burn in the oven. It's used as a decorative finish to add both sparkle and crunch to the tops of many baked goods. It's optional in most cases, but I do love it! Turbinado and demerara sugars, which are both versions of minimally processed cane or beet sugar, can be used as a substitute in a pinch.

I love organic and vegan sugars like monkfruit and coconut for my personal cooking and coffee drinking, but they can behave differently in some recipes. I suggest you stick to the standards for baking.

Do I Really Need a Candy Thermometer?

I will never tell you to spend your hard-earned cash on a useless gadget. I promise. But this inexpensive tool is really helpful for cooking sugar properly. (It will also make deep-frying a breeze.) Yes, you can drop bits of cooked sugar into cold water and check its texture to determine its stage, but by the time you've determined that, your sugar may have cooked to the next stage or even burned.

What are these "stages" all about? To make candy, you start by combining water and sugar over heat. The various stages, from thread to hard crack, refer to the final sugar concentration after most of the water has been cooked out. Using a candy thermometer takes all the guesswork out of the process.

Caramel Basics

In my opinion, caramel is the most magical substance to come from sugar. But it seems to make people the most nervous.

Cooking sugar breaks it down into glucose and fructose. Those molecules then break down further and react with one another, creating wonderful new flavor compounds. While ordinary sugar is simply sweet, caramel is buttery, bitter, malty, fruity, and toasty all at once.

Caramel can be made dry, with just granulated sugar (and a heavy-bottomed pot), or wet, with water added to the sugar. The former technique is a bit trickier. Without any water, the sugar will brown quickly and often somewhat unevenly. Swirling the pot with confidence should smooth it out and create a fluid caramel, but the process moves quickly. In most of my recipes, I call for water along with the sugar. The water encourages slow and even coloring, which makes the process easier to manage. Just be sure not to stir the sugar and water together or swirl the pot before the mixture starts to brown. Simply stand back and let it do its thing. Once you see the sugar browning in spots, then you can give the pot a gentle swirl.

Sugar will start to caramelize at around 340°F, but for a full-flavored caramel sauce, I like to cook it to somewhere around 365°F on a candy thermometer, or until it's a deep amber color, before adding the heavy cream. A light-colored pot makes these changes easier to spot, and using a candy thermometer to measure the temperature more accurately is always a good idea. If you're at all nervous about the caramel burning, keep a bowl of ice water by the stove. As soon as the caramel reaches the desired stage, set the pan in the ice water to instantly slow down the cooking process.

Crystallization is what happens when sugar crystals fall into the caramel, whether from the sides of the pan or from a sugary stirring spoon, and set off a chain reaction of crystal formation. The mixture starts to look grainy and opaque. Don't worry! Simply add a few tablespoons of water to the pan and continue to cook the mixture, swirling the pan occasionally but not stirring, until the caramel liquefies and smooths out again, then continue on. Viewed under a microscope, this caramel will not be as perfectly smooth and glossy as it would be had it never crystallized, but I'd rather that than throw out a pot of tasty caramel. (And who is looking at caramel under a microscope?)

As soon as your caramel reaches the correct color and temperature, it's time to remove it from the heat and use it right away for a recipe like Saffron and Cardamom Crème Caramel (page 124), or add heavy cream and butter to make a caramel sauce (page 52). When adding cream, go slowly and take care, as the caramel will bubble up and sputter at first. If you notice the caramel seizing up at all, just continue to stir it over the heat until everything is smooth and combined again.

Honeycomb Candy

MAKES ABOUT 6 CUPS

Honeycomb candy is super-easy to make, but it is essential to have all of the ingredients and necessary equipment at the ready. The process goes fast.

Enjoy this crumbled over ice cream or yogurt, on top of frosted cakes or cupcakes, or simply chow down standing up in the kitchen before your child gets home from school.

Butter for the pan

1 tablespoon (12 grams) baking soda

1 cup (200 grams) granulated sugar

6 tablespoons (128 grams) honey

½ teaspoon kosher salt

1 tablespoon (15 grams) water

This mixture is less likely to crystallize before it hits the right temperature than regular caramel because of the addition of honey, an invert sugar.

Line an 8- or 9-inch square pan with foil, leaving a 1-inch overhang on two opposite sides. Butter the foil and the exposed sides of the pan. Grab a small whisk, a heatproof spatula, a small plate, and an oven mitt, just in case, and set them by the stove.

Put the baking soda in a small bowl and set aside. In a large heavy-bottomed pot fitted with a candy thermometer, combine the sugar, honey, salt, and water. (The mixture will swell up to about four times the volume in the next step, so make sure the pot is big enough.)

Heat the sugar mixture to 300°F over medium-high heat, without stirring, about 5 minutes. Remove the pot from the heat, quickly remove the thermometer and place it on the plate, and immediately whisk in the baking soda. Take care to disperse the baking soda evenly, but don't mix for longer than a second or two, or you'll deflate the bubbles. Quickly scrape the mixture into the prepared pan. Don't touch it at all once it goes into the pan, so as not to disturb the bubbles. The mixture will swell up and then deflate a bit. Let it stand until cool

and hardened. To remove any hardened candy from your pot, simply fill the pot with water and set back on the stove. Bring the water to a boil, and the candy will dissolve. Throw your whisk and candy thermometer in there too, to remove hardened candy from them.

Remove the slab of candy from the pan and peel off the foil. Break the candy into pieces with your hands to serve.

The candy should keep its crunchy texture for at least a week stored in an airtight container at room temperature.

To easily line a baking pan with foil, first flip it over. Place the foil over the pan and mold it around the sides. Lift off the foil, maintaining its shape, and flip the pan back over. Then just ease the molded foil into the pan.

Bittersweet Caramel Sauce

MAKES ABOUT 1 CUP

Caramel can smell fear. Show it who's boss. Eventually you won't even need a recipe. For more caramel tips, see Caramel Basics, page 49.

- 2 tablespoons (30 grams) water
- ½ cup (100 grams) granulated sugar
- ⅔ cup (160 grams) heavy cream
- 2 tablespoons (¼ stick; 28 grams) butter
- 2 teaspoons pure vanilla extract
- ½ teaspoon kosher salt

Add the water to a small, heavy-bottomed pot. Pour the sugar into the center and cook, undisturbed, over medium heat until the caramel starts to darken in spots, 5 to 7 minutes. At this point, you can carefully swirl the pot to help smooth it out and brown more evenly. Continue to cook until the caramel is a deep amber, 1 to 2 more minutes.

Immediately add the cream and butter and stir to combine. Cook until the sauce is uniform and creamy, about 1 minute more. Stir in the vanilla and salt. Remove from the heat and let cool to room temperature, about 20 minutes. The sauce will thicken as it cools.

Store in an airtight container in the fridge for up to 2 weeks.

Use a light-colored heavy-bottomed pot for the best results: light-colored so that you can see the true color of your caramel and heavy-bottomed for even cooking.

Crystallization is the enemy of caramel, and cooks have devised various methods for preventing it. Some recipes say to wash down the sides of the pot with a wet pastry brush as the caramel cooks. Others suggest using a lid to create steam, which then condenses and washes down the sides of the pot. Some add lemon juice or corn syrup to the caramel. But I don't believe any of that is necessary. Just don't stir it before you need to. That's the key.

If you're using a thermometer, it should read 365°F.

**Giant Choco Chunkies
(page 59)**

**Chewy Chocolate Chip
Cookies (page 56)**

**Thin and Crisp Chocolate
Chippers (page 44)**

All-the-Chocolate Cookies

MAKES 9 BIG COOKIES

The large amount of sugar and the butter in this dough prevents the formation of gluten, which results in tender cookies. They also have a bit more brown sugar than white, which both makes them softer and works with the cocoa powder for a fudgier-tasting cookie.

For the absolutely best-tasting cookies, be sure to use good-quality chocolate that you'd want to eat out of hand. If you're not snacking on a bit of the chocolate in between stirs, you know you need to upgrade.

- 1 cup (136 grams) all-purpose flour
- ¾ cup (63 grams) Dutch-processed cocoa powder
- 1 teaspoon kosher salt
- ½ teaspoon baking powder
- ½ teaspoon baking soda
- 10 tablespoons (1¼ sticks; 141 grams) butter, at room temperature
- ¾ cup (150 grams) packed dark brown sugar
- ½ cup (100 grams) granulated sugar
- 1 large (50 grams) egg
- 2 teaspoons pure vanilla extract
- ½ cup (70 grams) milk chocolate, chopped
- ½ cup (70 grams) white chocolate, chopped
- ½ cup (70 grams) semisweet chocolate, chopped

Chopped bar chocolate, as opposed to chips, gives the cookies a more varied and interesting texture. Bar chocolate is also usually tastier, with a less waxy mouthfeel, than chips. Using a serrated knife makes easy work of chopping the chocolate.

In a medium bowl, whisk together the flour, cocoa powder, salt, baking powder, and baking soda. Set aside.

In a large bowl, with an electric mixer on medium speed or a wooden spoon, beat together the butter, brown sugar, and granulated sugar until creamy, about 3 minutes. Add the egg and vanilla and beat until well combined, scraping down the sides of the bowl as necessary.

With the mixer on low speed, add the flour mixture and beat just until combined. Add the chocolates and mix briefly to combine.

Tip the dough out, shape it into a square, and wrap well in plastic. Chill for at least 24 hours, and up to 36 hours.

Preheat the oven to 350°F. Line a baking sheet with parchment paper. Let the dough stand at room temperature for a few minutes to soften slightly.

Cut the dough into 9 equal pieces. Roll each piece into a ball. (At this point, you can freeze the dough balls in an airtight container for up to 3 months. Bake the cookies from frozen, but add a few extra minutes to the baking time.)

Arrange 5 of the balls on the prepared baking sheet and bake until set but still soft in the center, about 18 minutes. Transfer the cookies, still on the parchment paper, to a rack to cool. They will be delicate at first. Repeat with the remaining dough balls and a fresh parchment-lined sheet.

The cookies can be stored in an airtight container at room temperature for up to 3 days or frozen for up to 1 month.

Shaping the dough into a square before chilling it makes for easy portioning. You can simply cut the block into equal squares in a grid pattern instead of having to scoop balls out one at a time. The cookies will all be the same size and the mix-ins will be evenly dispersed.

Chewy Chocolate Chip Cookies

MAKES 24 COOKIES

These chocolate chip cookies have lovely crisp edges, soft middles, and a nice chew. The relatively large amount of granulated sugar contributes to the overall chewiness of the cookie, and because of that, they are also quite sweet. Resting the dough is imperative, as it allows the dough to develop deeper flavor.

3 cups (408 grams) all-purpose flour

1½ teaspoons baking soda

1 teaspoon kosher salt

20 tablespoons (2½ sticks; 283 grams) butter, softened

1½ cups (300 grams) granulated sugar

¾ cup (150 grams) packed dark brown sugar

2 large (100 grams) eggs, at room temperature

1 tablespoon (14 grams) pure vanilla extract

2½ cups (350 grams) semisweet chocolate disks

Use disks, not chips, here. The shape is better for cookies. Some of the disks will break as you mix the dough, creating smaller pieces. Once the cookies are baked, they will have well-dispersed little bits and large pools of melted chocolate that will mitigate their overall sweetness. Coarsely chopped bar chocolate would be fine too.

As for most cookies, I prefer salted or even cultured butter here but unsalted will work too.

In a medium bowl, whisk together the flour, baking soda, and salt.

In a large bowl, using a wooden spoon, mix together the butter, granulated sugar, and brown sugar until creamy. Add the eggs and vanilla and mix to combine, scraping down the sides of the bowl as necessary. Add the dry ingredients to the butter mixture and mix to combine. Mix in the chocolate disks.

Tip the dough out, shape it into a square, wrap well in plastic wrap, and chill for at least 8 hours, and up to 3 days.

Preheat the oven to 350°F, with the racks in the upper and lower thirds of the oven. Line two rimmed baking sheets with parchment paper.

Divide the dough into 24 equal pieces and roll into balls. (At this point, you can freeze the dough balls in an airtight container for up to 3 months. Bake the cookies from frozen, but add a few extra minutes to the baking time.)

Set 6 cookies on each prepared sheet, with at least 2 inches between them. Bake until the cookies are golden brown and just set in the center, about 12 minutes, rotating the sheets halfway through. Transfer the sheets to racks to cool for 10 minutes, then transfer the cookies to the racks to cool. Repeat with the remaining dough.

The cookies can be stored in an airtight container at room temperature for up to 3 days or in the freezer for 1 month.

Mix the dough by hand to avoid creaming the butter and sugar and creating loft. We're going for chewy here.

Despite the fact that it is very difficult to wait, cookie dough really does benefit from a rest. It gives the flour a chance to hydrate and the starches and proteins time to break down, so the baked cookies have a more developed flavor and an even brown color.

Avoid insulated baking sheets. They just don't conduct heat the same way as regular sheets and they often lead to underbaked or underbrowned cookies. Ditto for nonstick sheets, which can encourage too much browning.

Giant Choco Chunkies

MAKES 10 BIG COOKIES

I made a version for these for a Bon Appétit *video to re-create the very special cookies sold at Levain Bakery in New York City. These chunky chippers have dark chocolate, cherries, spice, and big whole walnut halves.*

16 tablespoons (2 sticks; 226 grams) cold butter, cut into cubes

1 cup (200 grams) packed dark brown sugar

¾ cup (150 grams) granulated sugar

2 large (100 grams) eggs (cold eggs are fine here)

4 teaspoons (19 grams) pure vanilla extract

3 cups (408 grams) all-purpose flour

1½ teaspoons ground cinnamon

1¼ teaspoons baking soda

1 teaspoon kosher salt

1¾ cups (245 grams) good-quality bittersweet or semisweet chocolate (do not use not chips), chopped

2 cups (186 grams) walnut halves

1 cup (145 grams) dried tart cherries

I use cold butter for these cookies. Cold butter doesn't cream as well with sugar as room-temperature, which means fewer air bubbles and less lift (and there's no waiting for the butter to soften). You want these guys to be pleasantly dense.

In a large bowl, with an electric mixer on medium speed, beat together the butter and both sugars until just creamy and combined. Beat in the eggs one at a time, scraping down the sides of the bowl as necessary. Add the vanilla, then add the flour, cinnamon, baking soda, and salt and beat to combine. Add the chocolate, walnuts, and cherries and beat to combine.

Tip the dough out onto a piece of plastic wrap. Pat it into a rectangle about 2 inches thick, wrap, and chill for 24 to 48 hours.

Preheat the oven to 400°F. Line a rimmed baking sheet with parchment paper. Let the dough stand at room temperature for a few minutes to soften slightly.

Cut the dough into 10 equal pieces. Roll each piece into a ball. (At this point, you can freeze the dough balls in an airtight container for up to 3 months. Bake the cookies from frozen, but add a few extra minutes to the baking time.)

Arrange 5 of the balls on the prepared baking sheet and bake until golden brown, about 14 minutes. If you press the cookies gently in the center, they should be slightly soft but not wet. Or, if you like the centers a little firmer, you can

bake the cookies for another 2 to 4 minutes. Let cool slightly on the pan on a rack before removing them. Repeat with the remaining dough. Serve warm.

The cookies can be stored in an airtight container at room temperature for up to 3 days or in the freezer for 1 month.

A long rest is ideal, but even an hour is better than nothing.

It's a little more time-consuming, but I prefer baking most cookies one sheet at a time. One sheet in the middle of the oven will always cook more evenly than two sheets on different racks.

I never use silicone baking mats for cookies, because they are too slick and result in too much spread.

Hazelnut Croquant Cookies

MAKES ABOUT 26 COOKIES

The word "croquant" means crisp or crunchy in French. While these egg white–based cookies are reminiscent of meringue, croquant cookies don't rely on whipped egg whites. Instead, all the ingredients are simply combined. The ratio of sugar to whites is much higher than in meringue. The result is a simple-to-make, delicate, crunchy cookie that's lovely eaten with a cup of tea.

2 large (60 grams) egg whites

1 cup (200 grams) granulated sugar

1¼ cups (160 grams) toasted and skinned hazelnuts, coarsely chopped

⅓ cup (45 grams) all-purpose flour

¼ cup (35 grams) bittersweet chocolate, chopped

1½ teaspoons pure vanilla extract

Pinch of kosher salt

Hazelnuts have a bitter papery skin that should be removed before using. Toast the nuts on a baking sheet at 350°F until the skins have started to separate from them, about 10 minutes. Immediately transfer the warm nuts to a dish towel, wrap them up into a pouch, and rub them around to remove most of the skins. It's OK if the nuts aren't completely clean.

Preheat the oven to 375°F. Line two rimmed baking sheets with parchment paper.

In a large bowl, stir together the egg whites and granulated sugar until creamy. Stir in the hazelnuts, flour, chocolate, vanilla, and salt.

Scoop about half the batter by 1-teaspoon scoops and place the scoops about 2 inches apart on one of the prepared baking sheets. Bake until the cookies are light golden brown and set, about 12 minutes. Transfer the sheet to a rack and let the cookies cool completely before removing them from the parchment. Repeat with the remaining batter and the other prepared sheet.

The cookies can be stored in an airtight container at room temperature for up to 1 week.

Burnt-Caramel Basque Cheesecake

Credit for this genius cheesecake goes to Santiago Riviera, pastry chef of La Viña Bar in San Sebastián, Spain. I've added a bit of dark caramel to the batter for more toasted sugar goodness.

Butter for the pan

3 tablespoons (45 grams) water

1½ cups (300 grams) granulated sugar

1½ cups (360 grams) heavy cream, at room temperature

5 large (250 grams) eggs, at room temperature

3 large (60 grams) egg yolks

2 pounds (904 grams) cream cheese, at room temperature

1 tablespoon (14 grams) pure vanilla extract

½ teaspoon kosher salt

3 tablespoons (26 grams) all-purpose flour

Cream cheese needs to be soft to be properly incorporated. I like to set it out on the kitchen counter the night before I make cheesecake to ensure that it's the correct texture.

When assembling the springform pan, set the bottom of the pan upside down in the ring, with the lip on the underside. That way, you won't have to fight with the lip of the pan when slicing your cake.

I always set heavy liquidy bakes on a rimmed baking sheet to make getting them into and out of the oven a little easier.

Preheat the oven to 425°F. Butter a 9-inch springform pan (the butter makes lining the pan easier) and line it with two crisscrossed pieces of parchment paper, with at least a 2-inch overhang all around. It's OK if the paper is wrinkled. Make sure you don't have any bare spaces at the bottom of the pan.

Add the water to a large heavy-bottomed pot, pour the sugar into the center, and heat over medium-high heat and cook, undisturbed, until the sugar dissolves and turns amber in spots, about 8 minutes. Carefully swirl the pot around to mix in the sugar, but do not stir. Then continue to cook until the sugar has become a deep amber caramel. Reduce the heat to low.

Stir in ¾ cup of the heavy cream. Be careful. The cream will sputter and steam and bubble up vigorously. Continue to heat the caramel, stirring, just until the mixture is smooth. Remove from the heat and let cool to room temperature. (The caramel will thicken slightly.)

In a medium bowl, whisk together the eggs and egg yolks. Set aside.

In the bowl of a stand mixer fitted with the paddle attachment, beat the cream cheese on medium speed until fluffy and creamy, about 2 minutes. Stop the mixer and add the cooled caramel, then beat until the mixture is smooth and well combined. Beat in the remaining ¾ cup cream, the vanilla, and salt. Beat in half of the egg mixture until combined, then beat in the remaining egg mixture. Sift the flour over the top of the batter and mix to combine.

Pour the mixture into the prepared pan and set the pan on a rimmed baking sheet.

Bake until the top of the cheesecake is dark brown and puffed and the cake is set about 1 inch in from the sides of the pan, 40 to 50 minutes. Loosely cover the cake with foil if necessary to prevent overbrowning as it bakes. When the cheesecake is done, the center will be set on top but still quite jiggly underneath. Set the pan on a rack to cool for at least 1 hour.

Serve the cheesecake at room temperature or refrigerate and serve chilled. Store leftovers, well wrapped, in the fridge for up to 3 days.

Caramel Pear Cobbler

SERVES 8

This recipe was inspired by Southern chef extraordinaire Virginia Willis's genius recipe for blackberry cobbler. Hers was the first I'd tasted where a lean cake batter was baked over fruit to create a multilayered, juice-soaked, pudding-like dessert with a lovely crisp top and stewed-berry bottom. In the past, I'd always topped my cobblers with biscuits, which is tasty, but that keeps the two entities a bit more separate. This version is like Virginia's but uses caramelized pears and a buttery cake layer to create the perfect one-pot fall indulgence.

PEARS

- 3 tablespoons (⅜ stick; 42 grams) butter
- 3 medium-firm Bosc pears, cored and cut into 8 wedges each
- 3 tablespoons (38 grams) dark or light brown sugar
- Pinch of kosher salt
- 1½ teaspoons pure vanilla extract

BATTER

- 8 tablespoons (1 stick; 113 grams) butter, melted
- 1 cup (200 grams) granulated sugar
- 1 cup (236 grams) buttermilk, at room temperature
- 1½ teaspoons pure vanilla extract
- 1 cup (136 grams) all-purpose flour
- 1 teaspoon baking powder
- ½ teaspoon baking soda
- ½ teaspoon kosher salt
- Crème Anglaise (page 97) for serving

Don't skip the crème anglaise. When it hits the hot cobbler, it swirls with the caramel-flavored pear liquor to create creamy layers of hot and cold, tart and sweet.

Preheat the oven to 350°F.

PREPARE THE PEARS. In a 10-inch ovenproof skillet, melt the butter over medium-high heat. Add the pears and spread them out into an even layer. Add the brown sugar and salt and cook until the pears are lightly browned in spots but not too soft and the caramel has thickened slightly, about 4 minutes. Transfer the pears to a plate and wipe out the skillet (no need to wash it).

PREPARE THE BATTER. In a large bowl, stir together the butter, sugar, buttermilk, and vanilla. Add the flour, baking powder, baking soda, and salt and stir to combine.

Add the batter to the skillet and spread it into an even layer. Top with the pears and any accumulated juices. Bake until the cake is set, about 45 minutes. You should be able to gently touch the cake in the center and feel that it's firm.

Serve big, warm scoops of cobbler topped with crème anglaise.

If the heat is too high, the caramel may separate. Fear not! Once the pears start cooking, they will release some juice and the whole mess will smooth out.

Sometimes the pears sink into the batter. Sometimes they don't. Either way, the cobbler will be great.

Lauryn's Hot-Sugar-Crust Peach Cake

SERVES 8

My friend and fellow food editor Lauryn Tyrell shared this recipe with me. As she promised, pouring hot water over the top of the cake before baking feels terrifying, but it produces an appealing crisp crust. In the oven, the sugar on the top of the cake melts into the water to create a very thin, crackly topping that is a delightful contrast to the soft, super-moist cake below.

6 tablespoons (¾ stick; 85 grams) butter, at room temperature, plus more for the pan

1½ cups (204 grams) all-purpose flour, plus 1 tablespoon (9 grams) for tossing

1½ teaspoons baking powder

1 teaspoon ground cinnamon

½ teaspoon kosher salt

1 cup (200 grams) granulated sugar

1 large (50 grams) egg, at room temperature

1 large (20 grams) egg yolk, at room temperature

1½ teaspoons pure vanilla extract

⅓ cup (75 grams) full-fat yogurt (not Greek)

1¼ cups (262 grams) chopped peaches, thawed frozen or fresh, peeled or not

¼ cup (60 grams) hot water

I find that frozen peaches are much more reliable than fresh. Just be sure to thaw them before using them for this recipe, or the cake will take too long to bake.

Preheat the oven to 375°F. Butter a 9-inch springform pan. Set the pan on a parchment-lined rimmed baking sheet.

In a medium bowl, whisk together the 1½ cups flour, baking powder, cinnamon, and salt. Set aside.

In another medium bowl, with an electric mixer on medium speed, beat the butter and ¾ cup of the sugar until light and fluffy, about 3 minutes. Add the egg and egg yolk and beat until combined. Beat in the vanilla. Add the flour mixture to the butter mixture, alternating with the yogurt, beating until just combined.

Toss half of the peaches with the 1 tablespoon flour and fold into the batter. Spread the batter evenly in the prepared pan. Top with the remaining peaches and sprinkle the remaining ¼ cup sugar evenly over the top. Drizzle the hot water over the sugar (most of it will dissolve).

Bake the cake until a cake tester inserted in the center comes out clean and the topping is crisp, about 40 minutes. Transfer the cake to a rack to cool completely.

To serve, remove the sides of the pan and lift the cake onto a serving plate. This cake is best the day it's made.

Some of the water may leak out of the springform pan, but that's what the baking sheet is there for.

Sweet Potato Crumb Muffins

MAKES 12 MUFFINS

Flour, melted butter, and brown sugar combine to make a crumb topping that is chewy and crisp, not soft. The brown sugar in the batter helps create a light and tender crumb and contributes to the muffins' moistness and gorgeous golden exterior. They're tasty and texturally satisfying, and they make a great self-contained breakfast that is perfect for feeding a hungry child while in transit on hectic school mornings.

CRUMB TOPPING

- ¾ cup (102 grams) all-purpose flour
- ½ cup (100 grams) packed dark brown sugar
- ¼ cup (29 grams) chopped pecans
- 1 teaspoon ground cinnamon
- Pinch of kosher salt
- 4 tablespoons (½ stick; 57 grams) butter, melted

MUFFINS

- 2 cups (272 grams) all-purpose flour
- 2½ teaspoons baking powder
- 1½ teaspoons ground cinnamon
- 1 teaspoon ground ginger
- ¼ teaspoon freshly grated nutmeg
- ½ teaspoon kosher salt
- ¼ teaspoon baking soda
- 8 tablespoons (1 stick; 113 grams) butter, at room temperature
- 1 cup (200 grams) packed dark brown sugar
- 2 large (100 grams) eggs, at room temperature

1½ cups (368 grams) roasted, peeled, and mashed sweet potatoes (from about 3 potatoes)

Roasting the sweet potatoes will produce the sweetest results, but really any way you cook them will be just fine—in the oven or microwave, or in boiling water.

Preheat the oven to 375°F. Line a standard 12-cup muffin pan with paper liners.

PREPARE THE CRUMB TOPPING. In a medium bowl, whisk together the flour, sugar, pecans, cinnamon, and salt. Add the melted butter and stir to combine. Set aside.

PREPARE THE MUFFINS. In a medium bowl, whisk together the flour, baking powder, cinnamon, ginger, nutmeg, salt, and baking soda.

In a large bowl, with an electric mixer on medium speed, beat the butter and sugar until fluffy, about 3 minutes. Beat in the eggs one at a time. Beat in the mashed sweet potato. Beat in the flour mixture. Do not overmix.

Divide the batter evenly among the muffin cups. Sprinkle the crumb mixture evenly over

the tops, squeezing it to create clumps of various sizes. (It's OK if some of the crumb mixture lands on the tin.)

Bake the muffins until they are puffed and set and a toothpick inserted into the center of one comes out clean, 26 to 30 minutes. Let the muffins cool in the pan on a rack for 10 minutes, then transfer to the rack to cool completely.

The muffins can be stored in an airtight container at room temperature for up to 3 days or in the freezer for up to 1 month. Thaw at room temperature.

I prefer light-colored pans for cakes and dark pans for muffins. Darker pans absorb heat more quickly than light pans. For cakes, that leads to dark, unpleasant edges. But for muffins, it means they dome nicely and brown evenly.

Use a large spring-loaded ice cream scoop to divide the batter evenly into the muffin cups.

Chocolate Peanut Butter Honeycomb Bars

MAKES ABOUT 12 PIECES

These live somewhere between millionaires' shortbread, Butterfinger candy bars, and peanut butter cups. The butter and the confectioners' sugar in the dough keep the crust nice and tender.

BASE

- 1¼ cups (170 grams) all-purpose flour
- ¼ cup (50 grams) granulated sugar
- 2 tablespoons (15 grams) confectioners' sugar
- ½ teaspoon kosher salt
- 10 tablespoons (1¼ sticks; 141 grams) butter, at room temperature

PEANUT BUTTER LAYER

- 1½ cups (384 grams) smooth natural peanut butter
- 1 cup (50 grams) crushed Honeycomb Candy (page 51)
- 6 tablespoons (45 grams) confectioners' sugar
- 1½ teaspoons pure vanilla extract
- ½ teaspoon kosher salt

TO FINISH

- 1¾ cups (245 grams) semisweet chocolate chips or chopped semisweet chocolate
- Broken pieces of Honeycomb Candy (page 51)

This is one of the only recipes where I condone the use of chocolate chips. Chips contain added soy lecithin to help them keep their shape when baked. For more precise pastry work, working with melted chips can be tricky, but here they are just fine. Use whatever you have—chips or bar chocolate.

Preheat the oven to 350°F. Line a 9-inch square baking pan with parchment paper, leaving a 2-inch overhang on two opposite sides.

PREPARE THE BASE. In the bowl of a food processor, combine the flour, granulated sugar, confectioners' sugar, and salt and pulse to mix. Add the butter and pulse until the butter is evenly distributed.

Tip the mixture into the prepared pan and spread into an even layer. Bake until the crust is just pale golden but set, 25 to 30 minutes. Let cool in the pan on a rack.

PREPARE THE PEANUT BUTTER LAYER. In a medium bowl, combine the peanut butter, honeycomb candy, confectioners' sugar, vanilla, and salt and stir to mix well. Spread in an even layer over the crust.

Melt the chips or chopped chocolate in short bursts in the microwave, stirring often. Drizzle the melted chocolate over the top of the peanut butter layer and smooth into an even layer. Scatter pieces of honeycomb candy on top. Chill until the chocolate is set, about 15 minutes.

Cut into 12 bars to serve.

The bars can be stored in an airtight container at room temperature for up to 1 week. (If it's very warm, you can store them in the fridge, but know that the humidity will cause the honeycomb to soften.)

You can butter the pan before you line it with parchment to keep the parchment in place while you spread out the shortbread dough. But that means the pan will be dirtier at the end. I usually prefer to wrestle with the paper a bit in order to spare myself a slighter harder washing job. Your choice.

Ginger Honey Cake

SERVES 8 TO 10

Together, fresh ginger and honey have dazzling potential. This cake is a good opportunity to use a special honey with a distinct flavor instead of the ubiquitous "honey bear" variety. I'm partial to Italian chestnut honey here.

1 cup (240 grams) neutral oil, plus more for the pan

¾ cup (256 grams) honey, plus about 2 tablespoons (43 grams) for glazing the cake

½ cup (100 grams) packed dark brown sugar

⅓ cup (47 grams) peeled and minced fresh ginger

2 large (100 grams) eggs, lightly beaten

2 cups (272 grams) all-purpose flour

2 teaspoons baking powder

¾ teaspoon kosher salt

Cream Cheese Ice Cream with Dates (page 135) for serving

With its high water content, honey adds both moisture and flavor to this cake. You can replace the honey with maple syrup, Lyle's Golden Syrup, or even molasses for a totally new cake.

I've written about peeling ginger with a spoon for every food magazine I've worked for, but that trick is tired. Who wants to whittle away at a stringy piece of ginger with a spoon? Buy the absolute fattest stalks of ginger you can find, and then you can comfortably use a vegetable peeler without worrying about waste. Or if the skin is fresh and relatively unblemished, you can mince the whole thing, skin and all.

Preheat the oven to 350°F. Grease an 8- or 9-inch round cake pan and line it with parchment paper.

In a large bowl, combine the oil, honey, and brown sugar and whisk until smooth.

Add the ginger and eggs to the honey mixture and stir to combine. Add the flour, baking powder, and salt and stir to combine.

Transfer the batter to the prepared pan and bake until a toothpick inserted into the center of the cake comes out with a few moist crumbs attached, 20 to 25 minutes. Transfer the pan to a rack to cool for about 10 minutes.

Flip the cake out of the pan onto another rack and brush with honey while it is still warm. Serve the cake warm or room temperature, with the ice cream.

The cake can be stored in an airtight container at room temperature for up to 3 days.

Lemony Hibiscus Doodles

MAKES 18 COOKIES

Along with the lemon zest, tart dried hibiscus flowers give the classic doodle some pucker power.

- 1½ cups (204 grams) all-purpose flour
- 1 tablespoon (6 grams) crushed dried hibiscus flowers
- 1 teaspoon cream of tartar
- ½ teaspoon baking soda
- ½ teaspoon kosher salt
- 10 tablespoons (1¼ sticks; 141 grams) butter, at room temperature
- ¾ cup (150 grams) granulated sugar
- 5 teaspoons (10 grams) finely grated lemon zest
- 1 large (50 grams) egg
- ½ teaspoon pure vanilla extract

TO FINISH

- ½ cup (100 grams) sanding sugar
- 2 teaspoons crushed dried hibiscus flowers

Cream of tartar keeps the sugar from crystallizing and gives the cookies their signature soft texture. For that reason, this is one of the few cookie doughs that doesn't benefit from a rest. Over time, the cream of tartar would become less potent and the cookies would not have their delightful chew.

Sanding sugar adds a bit of extra sparkle, but granulated would be fine in a pinch.

Preheat the oven to 375°F, with the racks in the upper and lower thirds of the oven. Line two baking sheets with parchment paper

In a medium bowl, whisk together the flour, hibiscus, cream of tartar, baking soda, and salt.

In a large bowl, with an electric mixer on medium speed, beat together the butter, sugar, and lemon zest until fluffy, about 2 minutes, scraping down the sides of the bowl as necessary.

Add the egg and beat until creamy, then beat in the vanilla, again scraping down the sides of the bowl as necessary. Add the flour mixture and beat on low speed until just combined.

In a small bowl, combine the sanding sugar and the hibiscus.

Divide the dough into 18 pieces and roll each piece into a ball. Roll each ball in the sugar mixture and arrange it on the prepared baking sheets, leaving at least 3 inches between balls.

Bake the cookies until just set and dry in the center, 10 to 12 minutes, rotating the sheets halfway through; do not overbake. Transfer the sheets to racks to cool for a few minutes, then transfer the cookies to racks to cool completely.

The cookies can be stored in an airtight container at room temperature for up to 5 days or in the freezer for up to 1 month. Thaw at room temperature before serving.

Passion Fruit and Pineapple Upside-Down Cake

SERVES 8

Take a trip to the tropics without ever leaving your kitchen.
A caramel made with butter and sugar is much more forgiving than a caramel made with just water and sugar, and it can be stirred as it cooks without worry. Use either dark or light brown sugar for the topping, depending on how pronounced you'd like the molasses flavor to be.

TOPPING

- 3 tablespoons (⅜ stick; 42 grams) butter
- ¼ cup (50 grams) packed light or dark brown sugar
- ¼ to ½ fresh pineapple, peeled, cored, and thinly sliced (170 grams)

CAKE

- 1½ cups (204 grams) all-purpose flour
- 1½ teaspoons baking powder
- ½ teaspoon kosher salt
- 1 cup (200 grams) granulated sugar
- 6 tablespoons (¾ stick; 85 grams) butter, at room temperature
- 1½ teaspoons finely grated lime zest
- 1 large (50 grams) egg
- ½ cup (120 grams) whole milk
- ⅓ cup (83 grams) passion fruit pulp (preferably with seeds)

Purple passion fruits, which are the only ones I can ever find in the United States, are ripe when their skin has wrinkled and shriveled. You can even hear the pulp slosh around in the center when you shake them. I like to buy them in bulk, let them all ripen, and then slice each one open and decant all the flesh into freezer bags to use whenever the fancy strikes. Store-bought puree is fine in a pinch, but when you take the flesh from the fresh fruit, you can keep the seeds, which add a pleasant crunch to baked goods.

Preheat the oven to 350°F.
PREPARE THE TOPPING. In 10-inch ovenproof skillet, melt the butter with the brown sugar over medium heat, stirring constantly until the mixture is smooth and cohesive. Remove from the heat.

Arrange the pineapple slices in concentric circles on top of the brown sugar mixture, overlapping them slightly. Set aside.

Remember that when you flip out the cake, the pineapple slices will be presented opposite of the way that you shingled them in the pan.

PREPARE THE CAKE. In a small bowl, whisk together the flour, baking powder, and salt.

In a large bowl, with an electric mixer on medium speed, beat the sugar, butter, and lime zest until fluffy, about 2 minutes. Beat in the egg. Add half of the flour mixture and beat to combine. Add the milk and passion fruit pulp and beat until combined, then beat in the remaining flour.

Carefully spread the batter in an even layer over the pineapple. Bake until the cake is golden brown and springs backs when pressed gently in the center, 35 to 40 minutes.

Let the cake stand on a rack for 5 minutes, then flip it out of the pan onto a serving plate. If any pineapple slices stick to the pan, simply release them with an offset spatula and return them to the top of the cake. Serve warm or at room temperature. The cake is best the day it's made, but you can store leftovers, well wrapped, in the fridge.

The lime zest is beaten with the butter because fat helps distribute flavor.

Downy Pumpkin Bundt
with Maple Cream

SERVES 10

Confectioners' sugar is pulverized granulated sugar. It's about ten times finer than granulated sugar, which is why we call it 10X in the biz. Cornstarch is usually added to the sugar as an anti-caking agent. In this recipe, it creates a soft and very finely textured cake.

CAKE

- 32 tablespoons (4 sticks; 452 grams) butter, at room temperature, plus more for the pan
- 3¼ cups (442 grams) all-purpose flour
- 1 tablespoon (12 grams) baking powder
- 2 teaspoons ground cinnamon
- ½ teaspoon ground ginger
- ¼ teaspoon ground allspice
- ¼ teaspoon freshly grated nutmeg
- 1 teaspoon kosher salt
- 1 pound (453 grams) confectioners' sugar
- 4 large (200 grams) eggs, at room temperature
- 1 tablespoon (14 grams) pure vanilla extract
- 1 15-ounce (425 gram) can pumpkin puree (about 2 cups)

MAPLE CREAM

- ½ cup (114 grams) mascarpone
- ¼ cup (78 grams) maple syrup
- ¼ cup (30 grams) confectioners' sugar
- 1 tablespoon (15 grams) whole milk if necessary

PREPARE THE CAKE. Preheat the oven to 350°F. Butter a 12-cup Bundt pan.

In a small bowl, whisk together the flour, baking powder, cinnamon, ginger, allspice, nutmeg, and salt.

In a large bowl, with an electric mixer on medium speed, beat the butter and confectioners' sugar until light and fluffy, about 5 minutes. Beat in the eggs one at a time, scraping down the sides of the bowl as necessary. Beat in the vanilla. Add the flour mixture and beat on low speed until just combined. Fold in the pumpkin.

Tip the batter into the prepared pan and smooth the top. Rap the pan on the counter to knock out any air bubbles. Bake until a skewer inserted into the center of the cake comes out clean, 70 to 75 minutes.

Transfer the cake to a rack and let cool in the pan for 15 minutes, then flip the cake out onto the rack and let cool completely.

PREPARE THE MAPLE CREAM. In a small bowl, stir together the mascarpone, maple syrup, and confectioners' sugar. Stir in a little milk if necessary to adjust the consistency; the cream should be thin enough for drizzling.

Drizzle the cream over the top of the cake to serve.

The best way to butter a Bundt pan is with a pastry brush and soft butter. Make sure to get into every ridge.

Rhubarb-Lime-Ginger Slab Pie à la Melissa

SERVES 10

I worked with chef Melissa Pellegrino at Fine Cooking magazine, where she once made a rhubarb, lime, and ginger jam that I have never been able to forget. This giant "Pop-Tart" is a homage to her and that exquisite confection.

Fresh rhubarb breaks down quickly when cooked, so using frozen rhubarb out of season is no sacrifice to texture. I like to buy all the fresh rhubarb I can get my hands on when it's available, chop it, and freeze it for later.

FILLING

- 5 cups (600 grams) chopped rhubarb
- 1 cup (200 grams) granulated sugar
- ¼ cup (32 grams) cornstarch
- 1 tablespoon (6 grams) peeled and minced fresh ginger
- 2 tablespoons (32 grams) fresh lime juice (from 1½ medium limes)
- 2 teaspoons finely grated lime zest
- Pinch of kosher salt
- 1 tablespoon (14 grams) cold butter, cut into small pieces

PASTRY

- Flour for rolling
- 2 recipes Laminated Butter Pie Pastry (page 5)

TO FINISH

- 1 large (50 grams) egg, lightly beaten

LIME GLAZE (OPTIONAL)

- 1¼ cups (150 grams) confectioners' sugar, sifted
- ½ teaspoon finely grated lime zest

- 1 teaspoon fresh lime juice
- 2 tablespoons (30 grams) heavy cream
- 2 tablespoons (30 grams) whole milk

One cup may seem like a lot, but sour rhubarb can take a lot of sugar.

I will never make you sift flour. But I will make you sift confectioners' sugar. I hate doing it. You'll hate doing it. But trust me, it's important for lump-free glaze.

PREPARE THE FILLING. In a medium saucepan, combine the rhubarb, sugar, cornstarch, ginger, and lime juice and bring to a boil over medium-high heat. Cook, stirring occasionally, until the rhubarb has softened and the liquid it releases has thickened, about 5 minutes. Remove from the heat and stir in the lime zest, salt, and butter.

Transfer the rhubarb mixture to a bowl, cover with plastic wrap, and refrigerate until cooled. (You should have about 2¼ cups filling.)

PREPARE THE PASTRY. Preheat the oven to 400°F.

On a lightly floured surface, roll one disk of dough out to a 10 x 12-inch rectangle. Transfer to a piece of parchment paper. Repeat with the remaining dough.

Transfer the piece of dough on the parchment, still on the paper, to a work surface. Top with the rhubarb filling, spreading it out evenly and leaving a 1-inch border all the way around.

Brush some beaten egg over all four edges of the dough. Top with the remaining rectangle of dough. Use a fork to crimp the edges together tightly. Use a sharp knife to trim ⅛ to ¼ inch of dough off the edges to even them. Use the parchment paper to lift the pie onto a rimmed baking sheet. Cut 4 small slits in the top sheet of dough for steam vents. Cover the pie and freeze for 15 minutes.

Brush the top of the pie with beaten egg. Bake until the pastry is deep golden brown and crisp, about 40 minutes. Transfer the pie, on the baking sheet, to a rack to cool.

PREPARE THE OPTIONAL LIME GLAZE. In a small bowl, whisk together the confectioners' sugar, lime zest and juice, heavy cream, and milk. Drizzle over the pie.

Stuffed S'more Cookies

MAKES 12 COOKIES

In these cookies, pulverized graham crackers become flour for a chewy cookie with a secret chocolate ganache center and toasty marshmallow hat.

Be sure to use stale marshmallows in these cookies. (Doesn't everyone have a half-empty bag in the back of their cupboard?) Over time, as they dry, the marshmallows become more firm and can withstand cooking a bit better. Fresh marshmallows tend to dissolve and slide off the cookies.

For even more toasted and caramelized sugar flavor, torch the top of the marshmallows when the cookies come out of the oven.

DOUGH

- 8 tablespoons (1 stick; 113 grams) butter, at room temperature
- ½ cup (100 grams) packed dark brown sugar
- ½ cup (100 grams) granulated sugar
- 1 large (50 grams) egg
- 2 teaspoons pure vanilla extract
- 1½ cups (173 grams) fine graham cracker crumbs (from about 12 crackers)
- 1 cup (136 grams) all-purpose flour
- ½ teaspoon baking powder
- ½ teaspoon ground cinnamon
- ½ teaspoon kosher salt

FILLING

- 3 tablespoons (45 grams) heavy cream
- ¾ cup (105 grams) semisweet or bittersweet chocolate, finely chopped
- ½ teaspoon pure vanilla extract
- Generous pinch of kosher salt

- 12 stale marshmallows, sliced in half

Using equal parts brown and white sugar makes these cookies soft in the centers and crisp on the edges.

You want the graham crackers to be very finely ground, like flour.

Don't skip the parchment paper here. As the marshmallows melt, they tend to slide around and make a sticky (but yummy!) mess, especially if they aren't stale.

PREPARE THE DOUGH. In a large bowl, combine the butter and both sugars and beat with a wooden spoon until smooth. Add the egg and vanilla and stir to combine, scraping down the sides of the bowl with a rubber spatula as needed. Add the graham cracker crumbs, flour, baking powder, cinnamon, and salt, and stir until a dough forms.

Transfer the dough to a large piece of plastic wrap and use the edges of the plastic to shape it into a flat 8-inch square that is about ½ inch thick. Chill until firm, at least 2 hours.

PREPARE THE FILLING. In a small saucepan, heat the cream until hot; or heat it in a bowl in the microwave. Don't walk away from the cream on the stovetop—cream loves to boil over when you're not looking.

Add the chocolate, vanilla, and salt to the hot cream and let stand for 2 minutes, then stir until smooth and uniform. (If not fully smooth, carefully heat it for a bit longer on the stovetop, stirring until smooth, or heat in the microwave in 5-second spurts, stirring after each blast, until smooth.)

Transfer the filling to a large piece of plastic wrap and use the edges of the plastic to shape it into a 4- to 6-inch square. Chill until firm, at least 2 hours.

Preheat the oven to 375°F. Line two rimmed baking sheets with parchment paper.

Cut the cookie dough into 24 equal pieces. Cut the chocolate filling into 12 equal pieces. (It's OK if the chocolate breaks a bit; just make sure you end up with 12 equal piles.)

Flatten one piece of dough slightly. Set a piece (or pile) of chocolate filling in the center and top with half of a marshmallow. Flatten another piece of cookie dough slightly and set it on top of the filling. Use your hands to shape the dough around the filling so it completely encloses it, and then roll it into a neat ball. Repeat with the rest of the dough and filling.

Evenly space 6 of the dough balls on each of the prepared baking sheets. Top each cookie with another marshmallow half. Bake one sheet until the cookies are set and relatively flat, with just-golden edges, 14 to 16 minutes. Let cool for 5 minutes on the baking sheet, then transfer to a rack to cool completely. Repeat with the second baking sheet of cookies. Run the flame of a kitchen torch over the top of each marshmallow to brown it slightly.

Serve the cookies warm or at room temperature.

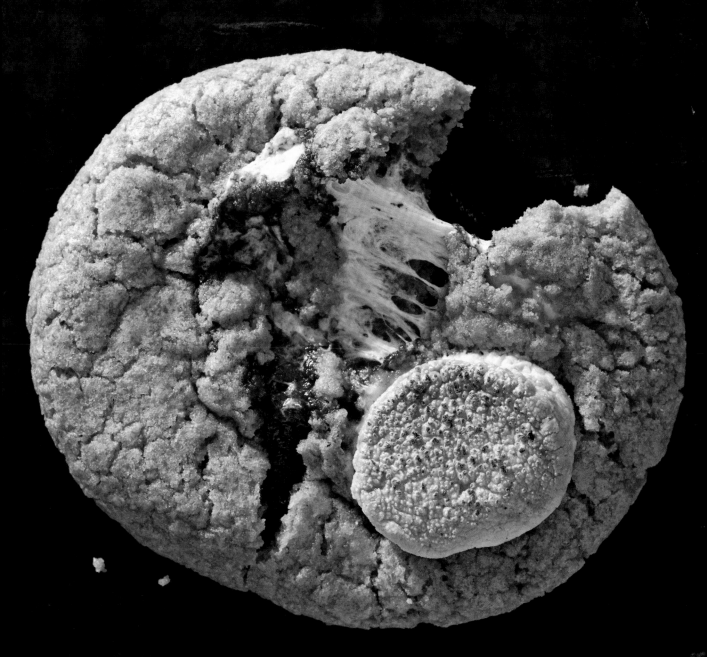

Caramelly Kettle Corn with Miso

MAKES ABOUT 16 CUPS

This umami-laced popcorn is smothered in more caramel than most kettle corn, but with a little less than caramel corn. I created it for the Goldilocks of sweet popcorn lovers: it's just right.

- 3 tablespoons (45 grams) neutral oil, plus more for the baking sheets
- ⅔ cup (150 grams) popcorn kernels
- 1½ teaspoons pure vanilla extract
- ¼ teaspoon baking soda
- 6 tablespoons (¾ stick; 85 grams) butter
- ½ cup (100 grams) granulated sugar
- ¼ cup (85 grams) Lyle's Golden Syrup or maple syrup
- 2 tablespoons (34 grams) white miso
- ¾ teaspoon kosher salt, plus more for sprinkling
- ½ teaspoon ground cinnamon

Preheat the oven to 250°F. Grease two large rimmed baking sheets or line them with silicone baking mats.

Add the oil and 2 popcorn kernels to a large heavy-bottomed pot, cover, and heat over medium heat until you hear those first kernels pop. Add the remaining corn kernels, cover, and cook, shaking the pot often, until the popping slows down; there should be a few seconds of silence between pops. Remove from the heat.

Transfer the popcorn to a large bowl. Discard any unpopped kernels. Set the vanilla and baking soda near the stove for easy access, along with a wooden spoon and a small plate.

In a small saucepan, combine the butter, sugar, syrup, miso, and salt and cook over medium heat until the butter is melted, stirring occasionally. Attach a candy thermometer to the side of

the pan and cook the mixture, undisturbed, until the temperature reaches 248°F, the firm ball stage.

Set the thermometer on the plate and remove the pan from the heat. Immediately stir in the vanilla and baking soda. The mixture will become foamy. Immediately pour it over the popcorn and use the wooden spoon to stir to coat it evenly.

Spread the popcorn out on the prepared pans. Bake until the coated popcorn is dry, 20 to 25 minutes, tossing occasionally. The popcorn will still be sticky. Sprinkle with a bit more salt and toss with the cinnamon.

Let the popcorn cool completely before serving or storing in an airtight container.

Baking soda will make the sugar mixture bubble up furiously. The key is to stir it in just enough to disperse it, but not so much that you destroy all the lightness it creates.

Eggs

The crackly, salty edges and runny, lush yolk of the perfect olive-oil-fried egg make me swoon. In fact, though, I'll eat eggs any which way. I wish my child felt the same. One of my earliest home videos of Arthur features him as a chubby-chinned, curly-haired cupid trying scrambled eggs, only to wince adorably, swallow, and try again, over and over, without ever changing his judgment. I laughed on the outside but cried on the inside. Eggs are usually such a savior when it comes to feeding children. Thankfully, he doesn't know how many eggs he's eaten over the years in the form of countless cakes and cookies.

Eggs do so much in baking. From airy meringues and tender soufflés to silky custards and ice cream, eggs deserve our undying love and appreciation. They add flavor, structure, and lift to baked goods. They both add moisture and help retain it, giving treats a longer shelf life. They make foods taste richer. And an egg wash applied before baking makes breads and pastries golden brown and glossy. And that's just whole eggs as they are. Once you separate them into yolks and whites, another universe reveals itself.

The Basics

I use large eggs for all my baking. I prefer organic free-range eggs. I'm convinced that they taste better, especially in custards and other eggy desserts, and I hope that the chickens that laid them are treated well. That said, organic or conventional, brown, white, or blue—it doesn't matter. As long as they are large eggs, they will work here. If you happen to buy medium- or extra-large eggs by mistake, as I've done on more than one occasion, simply follow the recipe according to weight. You can also use weights as a guide when you have leftover whites or yolks that you'd like to use up.

To crack an egg, I prefer to tap it against the rim of the bowl, along its equator, with confidence.

The idea is to make a clean break, so the eggshell can then easily be split in half. (Clean halves make separating an egg between the two pieces easier too!) Too gentle, and you'll create little shards that are likely to break the yolk or fall into whatever you are mixing. That's the same reason I don't like tapping the egg on the counter. That often only makes a dent, with dangerous little pieces, and rarely leads to a clean break.

It's much easier to separate eggs when they're cold, but they mostly perform better at room temperature. If you need to warm your eggs quickly, crack them into a bowl, then set the bowl in a larger bowl or pan of warm water. (Don't worry about combining the eggs first if the recipe directs

1 large egg white	=	30 grams	=	2 tablespoons
1 large egg yolk	=	20 grams	=	1 tablespoon
1 large whole egg	=	50 grams	=	3 tablespoons blended

you to add them one by one. Whole eggs will pour individually.)

Although it leads to more dirty dishes, when you need to separate multiple eggs, using three bowls is the safest method. Crack an egg into the first bowl. Use a slotted spoon or your hands to carefully transfer the yolk to another clean bowl. Pour the white into the third clean bowl. Then repeat as necessary. This way, if you do happen to break a yolk, you've only contaminated one egg white with yolk. Reserve that one for scrambling or another use, clean the bowl, and start again.

That said, a tiny bit of egg yolk won't necessarily ruin a foam, despite what everyone says. If a drop gets in there, don't fret. The whites will take a little longer to whip, but they should turn out just fine. If more than a drop or two of yolk contaminates a white, though, it would be best to start again.

Egg Yolks

Eggs yolks contain an emulsifier called lecithin. Lecithin bonds to both fats and water, which means it can combine ingredients that would usually repel each other. That helps distribute the fat evenly in a batter.

The lecithin also makes custards velvety. But overcooking or heating the egg yolks too aggressively will damage the emulsion that has been created and cause curdling. Adding cornstarch to a custard base can help by slowing the rate of coagulation, but it will change the texture of the custard. Think of vanilla pudding versus crème anglaise. Both are nice, but the latter is just a bit silkier. Baking a delicate egg custard in a water bath cooks it more slowly and evenly.

Egg Whites

Whipping egg whites unwinds their proteins. They then reconnect around air pockets to form bubbles that will expand in the heat of the oven. That's how desserts like soufflés and angel food cake rise. Adding sugar to the whites creates a denser, more stable foam because the sugar dissolves and coats the proteins in a sugar syrup. That's how you get a meringue.

Whites from older eggs tend to whip up a bit higher and faster than fresher ones, but the foam created by fresh whites is more stable. The takeaway: Don't worry about the age of your eggs. If they're not spoiled, they're perfect.

Most recipes have you whip the whites to either soft peaks or stiff peaks. Let's break that down a bit further:

SOFT PEAKS WITHOUT SUGAR: The foam should be smooth and spoonable. Pull the whisk out, and the peak will fall over itself. The peak will be a bit wider and a little less defined than in a foam made with sugar.

SOFT PEAKS WITH SUGAR: For a more stable foam, beat the egg whites until the yellowish tinge disappears and a very loose foam begins to appear before you add the sugar. If the sugar is added too early, the whites won't whip up as high. If it is added too late, the proteins can dry out and the bubbles won't be able to expand in the oven. Add the sugar slowly, about a tablespoon at a time, to ensure that it dissolves properly. Once all the sugar has been added, continue to beat the meringue until it is glossy and opaque. Pull the

Fresh Kiwi and Vanilla
Bean Cake en Croûte
(page 135)

whisk out, and the peak will hold but fall over at the tip.

STIFF PEAKS WITHOUT SUGAR: This is the trickiest stage to achieve when beating egg whites because there isn't any sugar to act as a buffer. If the egg whites are overbeaten and dry, they will look clumpy, like cumulus clouds. Those whites can't be folded into a batter properly, and they won't expand in the oven. Sometimes you can save overbeaten whites by beating in another white. That's a good save when you're making something like mousse. But if you need the egg whites to create lift, like in a soufflé, I'd recommend simply starting again. You're looking for a stable foam that will hold a small, straight peak, but it's always better to underwhip rather than overwhip. Stop and check the consistency often.

STIFF PEAKS WITH SUGAR: This stage is the easiest to attain. Again, don't start adding the sugar until you have a soft foam. Once all the sugar has been added, continue to beat the meringue until it is glossy and opaque. Pull the whisk out, and the peak will stay straight up.

I find that distinguishing between soft and stiff peaks can sometimes be hard because a big peak of meringue, when the whites have been beaten to stiff peaks, may still flop over at the top simply from its own weight. The key is to only pull out a small peak. If a small peak folds over, it's still at soft peak stage.

I don't use superfine sugar in my meringues. While it does dissolve more evenly, I find that granulated sugar provides more friction and a better whip.

If you have a copper bowl, beat the egg whites in it. The copper strengthens the proteins in the whites, enabling them to expand more, without collapsing. Added acid, like lemon juice and cream of tartar, have the same effect. And it's true that a lot of fat can ruin a good egg white foam, so thoroughly clean bowls and whisks are a good idea. But don't worry too much. Trace amounts of residual oil in a bowl are not enough to ruin anything.

To fold a meringue into a batter, use a balloon whisk rather than a rubber spatula. All of those little wires in a whisk behave like many rubber spatulas, cutting in the foam much faster and with much less deflation. Martha Stewart taught me this trick when I was working on her show *Martha Bakes*. If it's good enough for Martha, it's good enough for me.

Egg Wash

Brushed all over a pastry or a piecrust before baking, beaten egg, otherwise known as an egg wash or an egg glaze, results in a gorgeous, shiny, browned exterior. You can also use it to seal pastry or dough edges together.

To make an egg wash, I like using a whole egg plus 1 tablespoon heavy cream. The proteins in the egg and the cream help the baked good brown and the egg whites make it glossy. Although this is my favorite combination, you don't need to add anything to the beaten egg before you use it. You can also substitute milk or water for the cream, or you can use just an egg white or yolk rather than a whole egg. The results will be slightly less rich, but still lovely. The most important thing is to mix the egg wash very thoroughly so that it is a homogenous liquid, or you won't be able to brush it on evenly.

Meringue Kisses

MAKES ABOUT 50 KISSES

For pure kitchen magic, look no further than meringue. Egg whites and sugar whip up into ethereal clouds of confection perfection. I love the way a baked meringue stays firm in your hand but then melts softly on your tongue, like a snowflake.

There are three types of meringue: French, Italian, and Swiss. These kisses are made with a French meringue. Sugar is beaten into the egg whites and then baked. French meringue is baked at a low temperature for a long time to achieve crispness without adding any color. That said, a little color never hurt anyone, and I believe that lightly golden meringue tastes better, so don't worry too much about it!

The tapioca starch helps to prevent the tightening of the egg-white protein bonds, which could lead to shrinkage. Shirley O. Corriher, one of my baking heroes, uses tapioca starch instead of cornstarch in her meringues. She taught me, via her book BakeWise, *that tapioca starch swells at a lower temperature than cornstarch and more effectively prevents the tight coagulation of the proteins.*

½ lemon

4 large (120 grams) egg whites, at room temperature

Pinch of kosher salt

¼ teaspoon cream of tartar

1 cup (200 grams) granulated sugar

2 teaspoons tapioca starch

The acidic lemon juice and cream of tartar add insurance against graininess.

Cold eggs are easier to separate, but warm egg whites whip up better. So separate them when cold, but let them warm up before whipping.

Preheat the oven to 200°F. Line two rimmed baking sheets with parchment paper.

Rub the lemon half all over the inside of a large bowl. Add the egg whites, salt, and cream of tartar to the bowl and beat with an electric mixer on high speed until the mixture is foamy and you can no longer see any yellowish tinge, about 3 minutes.

Mix together the sugar and tapioca starch. With the mixer on, add the sugar mixture about 1 teaspoon at a time to the egg whites and then continue to beat until the whites are stiff, glossy, and you can't feel any sugar when you rub the mixture between your fingers. This will take a while! Don't rush. Once the meringue has reached stiff peaks, continue to beat for another few seconds to stabilize it and help keep it from deflating.

Transfer the meringue to a pastry bag fitted with a small star tip and pipe kisses (about 2 tablespoons each) onto the prepared sheets. They won't expand in the oven, so you can put them close together, about 25 kisses on each sheet.

Bake the meringues for 1½ hours, then turn off the oven and leave them in it until completely cool, at least 2 hours.

The kisses can be stored in an airtight container at room temperature for up to 1 week.

Basic Custard

MAKES 2 CUPS

My friend chef Thomas Joseph taught me this dreamy and lazy version of custard. I had spent years doing it the old-fashioned way: whisk together the sugar, cornstarch, and egg yolks, heat the milk, temper the eggs, and cook. He just dumps everything into a heavy-bottomed put and stirs away. Both ways work and one takes a lot less time. Guess which one I prefer?

- ¼ cup (50 grams) granulated sugar
- ¼ cup (32 grams) cornstarch
- Pinch of kosher salt
- 4 large (80 grams) egg yolks
- 2 cups (480 grams) whole milk
- 2 tablespoons (¼ stick; 28 grams) butter
- 1½ teaspoons pure vanilla extract

Cornstarch helps keep the eggs from curdling by slowing protein coagulation.

You can steep the milk with whatever flavorings you'd like—try smashed cardamom pods, cinnamon sticks, or vanilla beans. Then proceed with the recipe as written.

Set a fine mesh sieve over a medium bowl and set aside. In a medium heavy-bottomed saucepan, whisk together the sugar, cornstarch, and salt. Add the egg yolks and whisk to combine. Add the milk and whisk until smooth. Add the butter.

Cook over medium heat, whisking constantly, until the mixture just comes to a very low boil, about 5 minutes. (The target temperature for a cornstarch-thickened custard is 180°F. Use an instead-read thermometer to check the temperature if you have one.) Continue to cook the custard for another minute or two, then immediately pour it through the fine-mesh sieve; discard any solids in the sieve. Stir in the vanilla. Cover the custard with plastic wrap or wax paper pressed directly against the surface and refrigerate until cold. The custard can be refrigerated for up to 5 days.

A flat whisk is the perfect tool here. These whisks are able to get into the edges of the pan where cooked custard likes to hide (and scorch). If you don't have a flat whisk, use a regular French whisk along with a rubber spatula to scrape the edges.

Lime Curd

MAKES ABOUT 1 CUP

Lime curd, lemon curd's slightly sweeter sister, is essentially a citrus custard. Use it between cake layers (page 130), swirl into whipped cream, or just slather it on toast, along with some good ricotta cheese.

For lemon curd, swap the lime juice for lemon and increase the zest to 1 tablespoon.

4   large (80 grams) egg yolks

1   large (50 grams) egg

½   cup (100 grams) granulated sugar

½   teaspoon finely grated lime zest

½   cup (120 grams) fresh lime juice (from 4 to 5 limes)

6   tablespoons (¾ stick; 85 grams) butter, cut into pieces

Pinch of kosher salt

In a medium heavy-bottomed saucepan, whisk together the egg yolks, whole egg, and sugar until very well combined. Whisk in the lime zest and lime juice. Add the butter and salt. Heat the mixture over medium heat, stirring constantly with a wooden spoon, until it has thickened, about 5 minutes. You should be able to draw a clear line that holds through the curd on the back of the spoon. (An instant-read thermometer should register 170°F.) The curd will look thin at this point, but have faith! It will thicken as it cools. Immediately strain the curd through a fine-mesh sieve set over a small bowl; discard the solids in the sieve.

Press a piece of plastic wrap or wax paper directly against the surface of the curd and refrigerate until chilled. The curd can be refrigerated for up to 1 week.

A heavy-bottomed pot is important for even cooking here. Thin pans can lead to scorching.

More careful cooks make curd in a double boiler to heat the eggs very gently and avoid scrambling, but if you stir constantly and don't walk away, the curd should be just fine made in a heavy-bottomed saucepan. Little lumps and any bits of coagulated egg white will be strained out.

Pâte à Choux

"Choux" means cabbage in French, which I think makes this dough the cutest around. Choux pastry is cooked twice: once on the stovetop and then again in the oven. First the butter, sugar, salt, water, and flour are cooked together on the stove. This step thickens the mixture by gelatinizing the starch. Once the mixture has cooled a bit, the eggs are beaten in. The eggs provide the moisture needed to puff the dough in the hot oven. Along with the butter, the fat in the eggs also helps give the puffs their signature crisp, golden exterior.

Master this easy dough, and you'll never have to go a day without cream puffs. A dream life.

6 tablespoons (¾ stick; 85 grams) butter, cut into pieces

2 teaspoons granulated sugar

½ teaspoon kosher salt

¾ cup (180 grams) water

¾ cup (102 grams) all-purpose flour

3 large (150 grams) eggs

This dough relies on steam created in the oven to puff it up, so it's key to preheat the oven properly.

Ideally the butter will fully melt and the water will come up to a boil at the same time so that too much water doesn't evaporate, but don't worry about it. Chefs often claim that this dough is harder to make than it is. Yes, you don't want to lose much water, but as long as you don't leave the kitchen to take a nap or something, you should be fine.

Preheat the oven to 400°F, with the racks in the upper and lower thirds of the oven. Line two rimmed baking sheets with parchment paper.

Combine the butter, sugar, salt, and water in a medium saucepan and bring to a simmer over medium heat, stirring with a wooden spoon. As soon as the mixture comes to a simmer add the flour, stirring constantly, and stir until the dough forms a ball and pulls away from the sides of the pan, about 1 minute. Remove the pan from the heat and let the dough cool for 3 to 4 minutes, stirring occasionally.

One at a time, add the eggs to the dough, stirring vigorously after each addition with the wooden spoon. The dough will break apart and slide around in the pan, but then it will come back together.

Drop the dough by 2-tablespoon scoops about 3 inches apart onto the prepared sheets, about 9 per sheet. (A small ice cream scoop makes this easy and fast.) With a damp fingertip, tap down any peaks. (You can also freeze the shaped dough to bake later. Once firm, transfer to an airtight container and store in the freezer for up to 1 month. Just bake from frozen when you're ready. The puffs will take an extra couple of minutes in the oven.)

Bake until the puffs are deep golden brown and puffed, 22 to 26 minutes, rotating the sheets halfway through. Transfer the sheets to racks, pierce the side of each puff with a toothpick to allow steam to escape, and let cool completely. Store in an airtight container at room temperature for up to 3 days.

Choux pastries must be baked through, or they will collapse after cooling. They should be golden brown, feel light for their size, and sound hollow when you tap the underside.

Crème Anglaise

MAKES 1¾ CUPS

This thin custard makes everything you pour it over better. It adds richness, moisture, sweetness, and creaminess to sliced fruit, less-than-fresh cake, and cobbler (page 64). It can even serve as an excellent upgrade to milk for cookie dunking.

¾ cup (180 grams) heavy cream

¾ cup (180 grams) whole milk

4 large (80 grams) egg yolks

¼ cup (50 grams) granulated sugar

½ teaspoon kosher salt

Crème anglaise is thickened with egg yolks alone. Without starch, it's a bit fussier and more prone to curdling. For the faint of heart, I suggest making it in a double boiler the first couple of times. If you don't have a double boiler, set a large heatproof bowl over a pot of barely simmering water, making sure that the bottom of the bowl doesn't touch the water. Once you feel comfortable with the technique, you can give it a go directly on the stovetop. Just be sure to stir gently and constantly. Don't leave it unattended for even a moment.

Set a fine-mesh sieve over a medium bowl. In a small saucepan, whisk together the heavy cream, milk, egg yolks, sugar, and salt and cook over medium heat, stirring with a wooden spoon, until the custard has thickened slightly, about 3 minutes. (An instant-read thermometer should register between 160°F and 170°F.) You should be able to draw a clear line through the custard on the back of the wooden spoon. Immediately pour through the prepared fine-mesh sieve.

Cover the custard with plastic wrap pressed directly against the surface and refrigerate until cold. The crème anglaise can be refrigerated for up to 3 days.

To prevent a skin forming while the crème anglaise cools, press plastic wrap directly against the surface. Or, top it with a bit of melted butter.

Vanilla Bean–Roasted Stone-Fruit Eton Mess

Tart, sweet, crunchy, and creamy—the varying textures of the crushed meringue, cool whipped cream, and stewed fruit create a dessert that's both simple and profound in its deliciousness. Roasting the fruit converts less-than-perfect specimens into something worth eating. Water evaporates, flavors intensify, and sugars caramelize.

1½ pounds stone fruit (peaches and plums, etc.), halved, pitted, and cut into wedges

¼ cup (50 grams) granulated sugar

1 vanilla bean, split lengthwise and seeds scraped out and reserved

2 teaspoons fresh lemon juice

5 ounces (140 grams) store-bought meringue kisses or ½ recipe Meringue Kisses (page 90)

3 cups (720 grams) cold heavy cream

2 tablespoons (15 grams) confectioners' sugar

You can swap in a tablespoon of pure vanilla extract for the vanilla bean seeds if necessary, but don't add it until after cooking the fruit for maximum impact.

Preheat the oven to 400°F. Line a rimmed baking sheet with parchment paper.

Put the fruit on the prepared baking sheet, toss with the sugar and vanilla bean seeds, and bake until the sugar has begun to caramelize and the fruit is soft, about 15 minutes. Remove from the oven and set aside to cool.

Mash the roasted fruit with a fork; the mixture doesn't need to be completely smooth. (You should have about 2½ cups.) Add the lemon juice.

Put the meringue kisses in a large resealable plastic bag. Use a rolling pin to lightly crush the cookies. (You want pieces of varying sizes.)

In a large bowl, combine the cream and confectioners' sugar and beat with an electric mixer on medium-high speed until the cream holds stiff peaks. Fold the crushed meringue into the whipped cream.

Starting and ending with the fruit mixture, layer the fruit and the cream mixture in individual serving dishes, creating as many layers as you like. Serve immediately.

Mini Pavlovas with Tahini Cream and Mango

SERVES 8

Pavlova is an elegant dessert of a baked meringue topped with cream and fruit. Here the individual meringues are baked at a low temperature for a long time to give them a crisp exterior and a marshmallowy interior. Don't worry too much about color: a little browning will only add more flavor.

As a South Asian American, I am genetically predisposed to sniff out the most gorgeous mangoes that exist. You too should literally sniff them at the grocery store. Zero aroma equals zero flavor. Gorgeous ripe, fragrant mango slices are heavenly paired with sweet and nutty tahini cream.

1 recipe meringue for Meringue Kisses (page 90)

TAHINI CREAM

½ cup (112 grams) tahini

2 tablespoons (25 grams) light or dark brown sugar

2 teaspoons pure vanilla extract

1 cup (240 grams) heavy cream, plus a bit more if necessary

TO FINISH

1 large ripe mango, peeled and thinly sliced

1 tablespoon (13 grams) granulated sugar if necessary

Sesame seeds for sprinkling

Tahini tends to separate as it sits. Make sure to thoroughly combine it before measuring. An immersion blender works well.

Preheat the oven to 200°F. Line two rimmed baking sheets with parchment paper.

Using a large ice cream scoop, portion the meringue into 8 mounds on the baking sheets, 4 per sheet. Using the back of a spoon, make a small divot in the center of each mound.

Bake the meringues for 1½ hours, then turn off the oven and leave the meringues in it until completely cool, at least 2 hours.

PREPARE THE TAHINI CREAM. In a small bowl, combine the tahini, brown sugar, and vanilla. In a large bowl, beat the cream with an electric mixer on medium to medium-soft peaks.

Fold the tahini mixture into the whipped cream. (You should have about 3 cups.) If the cream stiffens too much, gently fold in an extra teaspoon or so of heavy cream.

If the mango isn't too sweet, toss it with the granulated sugar.

Arrange the meringues on a serving platter. Top each meringue with some of the cream and mango and sprinkle with sesame seeds. Serve immediately.

Chocolate and Coconut Meringue Cookies

MAKES ABOUT 30 COOKIES

Melted chopped bar chocolate is much better for dipping than melted chocolate chips. The stabilizers in chips make the melted chocolate too thick. It's not essential to temper the chocolate, but the cookies will hold better and the chocolate will look nicer if it is. For instructions on my favorite tempering method, see page 148.

½ lemon

4 large (120 grams) egg whites, at room temperature

Pinch of kosher salt

¼ teaspoon cream of tartar

1 cup (200 grams) granulated sugar

2 teaspoons tapioca starch

¼ cup (21 grams) cocoa powder (Dutch-processed or natural)

2 tablespoons (15 grams) confectioners' sugar

1 cup (76 grams) toasted unsweetened shredded coconut

TO FINISH

1½ cups (210 grams) bittersweet chocolate, melted

1 to 2 teaspoons coconut oil, melted, if necessary

Toasted unsweetened shredded coconut for sprinkling

Use whichever type of cocoa powder you have on hand. Either will work in this recipe. That said, I prefer the darker color and mellower flavor of Dutch-processed cocoa here.

Bittersweet chocolate tames the sweetness of the meringue.

Line two rimmed baking sheets with parchment paper.

Rub the lemon half all over the inside of a large metal bowl. Add the egg whites, salt, and cream of tartar and beat with an electric mixer on high speed until the whites are foamy and you can no longer see any yellowish tinge, about 3 minutes.

Mix together the sugar and tapioca starch. With the mixer running, add the sugar mixture about 1 teaspoon at a time to the egg whites, then continue to beat until the whites are stiff and glossy. This will take a while! Don't rush. Once you've added all the sugar, continue to beat the whites until you can't feel any sugar when you rub some meringue between your fingers, about 15 minutes. Sift the confectioners' sugar and cocoa over the meringue and fold them in with a balloon whisk. Gently fold in the coconut.

Transfer the meringue mixture to a pastry bag fitted with a large star tip (such as Ateco #823) and pipe small spirals, at least 2 inches apart, on the prepared sheets, about 15 per sheet. Let the meringues stand at

room temperature, uncovered, until they are no longer sticky to the touch, 60 to 90 minutes.

Preheat the oven to 350°F.

Bake the cookies, one sheet at a time, until they are slightly puffed, crisp, and dry, about 17 minutes. Let the cookies stand on the sheets until cool.

Set the melted chocolate in a small glass or bowl.

Dip each cookie in chocolate, then return it to the baking sheet. If the melted chocolate is too thick and doesn't easily coat the cookies, stir in a little bit of the coconut oil. Sprinkle the chocolate with some shredded coconut.

Let the cookies stand at room temperature until set. Store these guys in an airtight container for up to a week, and keep them away from moisture!

Letting the meringues stand gives them a chance to firm up and form a skin. This will help them puff up in the oven.

For dipping, I like to transfer the melted chocolate to a rocks glass or something similar (you may have to do it in batches). The glass is tapered, so the chocolate stays pooled at the bottom while the mouth is wide, both of which make for easy dipping.

Caramelized Banana Custard Cornflake Tart

SERVES 8 TO 10

This dazzling tart was inspired by my boring weekday breakfast. Cornflakes became a sweet crust that's both chewy and crisp. Milk was transformed into a silky custard filling, and the bananas got a heat treatment for more complex flavor. This tart isn't technically breakfast food, but I would be happy to start my day with a healthy slice.

CRUST

- 1½ cups (54 grams) finely crushed (but not powdered) cornflakes
- ¼ cup (50 grams) granulated sugar
- 8 tablespoons (1 stick; 113 grams) butter, melted and cooled, plus more for the pan
- Large pinch of kosher salt

CUSTARD

- ¼ cup (50 grams) granulated sugar
- 3 tablespoons (24 grams) cornstarch
- 4 large (80 grams) egg yolks
- ½ teaspoon kosher salt
- 2 cups (480 grams) whole milk
- ½ cup (120 grams) heavy cream
- 2 tablespoons (¼ stick; 28 grams) butter
- 2 teaspoons pure vanilla extract
- ¼ teaspoon pure almond extract

TO FINISH

- 3 to 4 large bananas, sliced
- Granulated sugar for sprinkling
- Whipped cream for serving

PREPARE THE CRUST. Preheat the oven to 350°F. Line a 9-inch square baking pan with foil, leaving a 2-inch overhang on two opposite sides.

In a large bowl, combine the cornflake crumbs, sugar, butter, and salt and mix well. Transfer the crumb mixture to the prepared pan and press the crumbs evenly over the bottom.

Bake until the crust is fragrant and set, 25 to 30 minutes. Remove from the oven and let cool completely.

MEANWHILE, PREPARE THE CUSTARD. In a medium heavy-bottomed saucepan, whisk together the sugar, cornstarch, egg yolks, and salt. Add the milk and cream and whisk to combine. Add the butter. Bring the mixture to a low boil over medium heat and cook, whisking constantly, until the custard has thickened, about 8 minutes. Make sure the custard boils for at least 1 minute before removing it from the heat. Stir in the vanilla and almond extracts.

Pour the custard through a fine-mesh sieve into the prepared crust. Cover with plastic or wax paper pressed directly against the surface and refrigerate for at least 4 hours, and up to overnight.

Just before serving, top the tart with the slices of banana arranged in a decorative pattern. Sprinkle with sugar and use a kitchen torch to caramelize the sugar. If the custard softens too much under the heat of the blowtorch, pop it back into the fridge for about 10 minutes.

Use the foil overhang to transfer the tart from the pan to a cutting board. Cut into squares and serve immediately, topped with whipped cream. The tart is best the day it's made. Store leftovers in the fridge.

Please invest in a kitchen blowtorch! This inexpensive tool is the key to unlocking the flavor-enhancing abilities of caramelization.

Use a flat-bottomed measuring cup to press the crumbs into an even crust.

Cornstarch needs a minute or two at about 200°F to gelatinize, or swell and absorb water, properly.

Chocolate Cherry Cream Cake

SERVES 10 TO 12

It may sound a little dated, but chocolate and cherry never goes out of style.

CAKE

- ⅔ cup (160 grams) neutral oil, plus more for the pans
- 2½ cups (340 grams) all-purpose flour
- 1 teaspoon baking soda
- 1 teaspoon kosher salt
- ¾ cup (63 grams) Dutch-processed cocoa powder
- 1 cup (240 grams) coffee, cooled slightly
- 1 cup (236 grams) buttermilk
- 2 large (100 grams) eggs
- 2 teaspoons pure vanilla extract
- 2 cups (400 grams) granulated sugar

COMPOTE

- 3 cups (389 grams) pitted sweet or sour cherries, frozen but not thawed
- 2 tablespoons (25 grams) granulated sugar
- 2 teaspoons cornstarch

MOUSSE

- 12 tablespoons (1½ sticks; 170 grams) butter, at room temperature
- ¾ cup (150 grams) granulated sugar
- Pinch of kosher salt
- 2 teaspoons pure vanilla extract
- ¾ cup (105 grams) bittersweet chocolate, melted and cooled slightly
- 3 large (150 grams) eggs

GLAZE

- 2⅓ cups (327 grams) semisweet chocolate, chopped
- 1 tablespoon (15 grams) neutral oil
- Pinch of kosher salt
- 1 cup (240 grams) heavy cream

You can make the mousse in advance and refrigerate it, covered, for up to 24 hours. To soften it again, transfer it to the bowl of a stand mixer fitted with the paddle attachment and beat it slowly while aiming a hair dryer at the bottom of the bowl intermittently to warm it.

To test a cake for doneness without using a toothpick, simply press it gently in the center. It should feel firm to the touch and spring back. If your finger leaves an indentation, or you hear a faint little crackling sound when you press, bake the cake for a few minutes more.

MAKE THE CAKE. Preheat the oven to 350°F. Grease two 8-inch round cake pans and line with parchment.

In a large bowl, whisk together the flour, baking soda, and salt.

In a medium bowl, whisk together the cocoa powder and coffee. Add the oil, buttermilk, eggs, vanilla, and sugar and whisk until smooth. Whisk half of the wet mixture into the dry ingredients until combined, then stir in the rest of the wet mixture.

Divide the batter between the prepared pans and bake until a toothpick inserted into the center of one cake comes out with a few moist crumbs attached, 35 to 40 minutes. Transfer the pans to a rack and let cool slightly, then remove the cakes from the pans and transfer to a rack, still on the parchment so that they don't stick to the rack, to cool completely.

MEANWHILE, MAKE THE COMPOTE. In a small saucepan, combine the cherries, sugar, and cornstarch. Cook over medium-high heat, stirring and smashing the cherries as they soften, until the mixture is jammy and thick, about 4 minutes. Remove from the heat and set aside to cool completely.

MAKE THE MOUSSE. In a large bowl, with an electric mixer on medium speed, beat the butter and sugar together until light and fluffy, about 4 minutes. Beat in the salt and vanilla. Beat in the

continues

chocolate. Then add the eggs one at a time, beating until well combined after each addition.

ASSEMBLE THE CAKE. Trim the domed top from each cake layer and then carefully split each one into two equal layers (see Splitting a Cake, below).

Set one layer, cut side up, on a serving plate. Spread one third of the cherry compote over the top and then spread a generous ½ cup of the mousse over that. Top with another cake layer and spread with another third of the compote and a generous ½ cup mousse. Repeat with the third layer, the remaining compote, and another generous ½ cup mousse. Finish with the final layer, cut side down, on top.

Spread the remaining mousse over the top and sides of the cake. Cover the cake and chill until firm, at least 2 hours.

PREPARE THE GLAZE AND FINISH THE CAKE. In a medium bowl, combine the chocolate, oil, and salt; set aside.

In a small saucepan, bring the cream to a simmer over medium-low. Remove the pan from the heat, pour the cream over the chocolate mixture, and let stand for 3 minutes. Whisk until smooth.

Spread the glaze evenly over the top and sides of the cake.

Serve the cake at room temperature. Store any leftovers, well wrapped, in the fridge for up to 3 days.

SPLITTING A CAKE

To split a cake layer evenly, start by inserting toothpicks all around the sides of the layer, exactly halfway between the top and bottom, at about 2-inch intervals. Use a serrated knife to cut through the layer, using the toothpicks as a guide. The tendency to aim the knife upward as you cut around is strong. Keep that in mind, and be sure to keep the knife parallel to the work surface for a level cut. Remove the toothpicks.

Chocolate Brûlée Tart

SERVES 8

The elegant chocolate custard would be delicious on its own, but it gets a flavor boost from the toasted hazelnuts in the crust and the crackly caramelized sugar top.

CRUST

- 1 cup (136 grams) all-purpose flour
- ½ cup (66 grams) toasted and skinned hazelnuts
- 2 tablespoons (25 grams) granulated sugar
- ½ teaspoon kosher salt
- 8 tablespoons (1 stick; 113 grams) cold butter, cut into cubes
- 3 tablespoons (45 grams) ice water
- 1 large (30 grams) egg white, beaten

FILLING

- ¾ cup (180 grams) whole milk
- 1 cup (240 grams) heavy cream
- 1 large (50 grams) egg
- 4 large (80 grams) egg yolks
- 2 tablespoons (25 grams) granulated sugar
- Pinch of kosher salt
- 1¼ cups (175 grams) bittersweet chocolate, melted and cooled slightly
- 2 teaspoons pure vanilla extract
- ½ teaspoon espresso powder

TO FINISH

- ¼ cup (50 grams) granulated sugar

Whizzing the hazelnuts with the sugar makes it easier to process the hazelnuts into fine crumbs without turning them into hazelnut butter.

If you chilled the tart pan on a baking sheet, make sure to swap the sheet out with one that is at room temperature before baking. A cold sheet will affect the bake on your tart shell.

You want to give the tart shell a good, deep blind-bake so that it stays crisp under the custard filling.

PREPARE THE CRUST. In the bowl of a food processor, combine the flour, hazelnuts, sugar, and salt and process until the hazelnuts are finely ground. Add the butter and pulse until the mixture resembles coarse meal with some slightly bigger pieces of butter. Add the water and pulse just until the dough is evenly moistened.

Tip the dough out onto a sheet of plastic wrap and use a bench scraper to lift and fold the dough over itself once or twice, or until it comes together. Wrap in the plastic wrap and shape into a flat disk. Refrigerate the dough for at least 1 hour, and up to 2 days.

On a lightly floured surface, roll the dough out to about an 11-inch circle. Transfer to a 9-inch fluted tart pan with a removable bottom, ease the dough into the corners, and run a rolling pin over the top edge to trim the excess dough. Freeze the tart shell for 15 minutes.

Preheat the oven to 375°F.

Line the frozen shell with parchment paper and fill it completely with pie weights, dried beans, or rice. Set on a rimmed baking sheet and bake until the crust under the paper is dry and set (carefully lift up the paper to check), about 20 minutes. Remove the paper and weights and brush the crust with the egg white. Return it to the oven and bake until the crust is golden brown, another 25 minutes or so. Remove from the oven and set aside. Reduce the oven temperature to 300°F.

PREPARE THE FILLING. In a medium saucepan, heat the milk and cream until hot. Remove from the heat.

In a medium bowl, whisk together the egg, egg yolks, sugar, and salt until completely homogenous. Add the warm cream mixture to the egg mixture, whisking constantly.

continues

Whisk in the chocolate, vanilla, and espresso powder. Pour the mixture through a fine-mesh sieve into the prepared crust.

Bake the tart until the filling is just set but still has a bit of jiggle in the center, about 25 minutes. Remove from the oven and let cool completely. Then cover and refrigerate until cold, at least 4 hours, and up to overnight.

Just before serving, remove the tart ring and transfer the tart to a serving plate. Sprinkle about half of the sugar over the top and use a kitchen torch to caramelize it. Add the remaining sugar and repeat the process. Let stand until the sugar has cooled and hardened, about 5 minutes, then serve immediately.

Store leftovers in the fridge for up to 3 days. The brûléed topping will soften over time.

Be sure to fill the unbaked tart shell all the way up to the very top with pie weights. If necessary, supplement store-bought weights with dried beans or rice so that you can fill the shell completely.

Chocolate Chestnut Loaf

Earthy, buttery-sweet chestnuts make a lovely complement to the cocoa in this pretty loaf. Dutch-processed cocoa powder has been treated to reduce the cocoa's natural acidity. I prefer it to natural cocoa powder because it has a deeper chocolate flavor with less fruitiness.

Butter for the loaf pan

1½ cups (204 grams) all-purpose flour

1 teaspoon kosher salt

1 teaspoon baking powder

½ teaspoon baking soda

1½ cups (300 grams) granulated sugar

½ cup (120 grams) neutral oil

2 teaspoons pure vanilla extract

2 large (100 grams) eggs

½ cup (120 grams) sour cream

1 cup (150 grams) cooked chestnuts

3 tablespoons (45 grams) heavy cream

¼ cup (22 grams) Dutch-processed cocoa powder, sifted

You can use plain full-fat yogurt, crème fraîche, or full-fat cottage cheese in place of the sour cream.

Look for packaged peeled steamed chestnuts near the dried fruit in the supermarket.

Preheat the oven to 375°F. Butter an 8½ x 4½-inch loaf pan and line it with parchment, leaving a 2-inch overhang on the two long sides.

In a medium bowl, whisk together the flour, salt, baking powder, and baking soda; set aside.

In a large bowl, whisk together the sugar, oil, vanilla, eggs, and sour cream. Fold the dry ingredients into the egg mixture until just combined. Transfer half the batter to a medium bowl.

In a small bowl, using an immersion blender, combine the chestnuts and heavy cream and blend until smooth. (A regular blender also works. Just be sure to scrape out every drop of chestnut cream from the blender jar.) Add the chestnut cream to one half of the batter and blend well.

Add the cocoa powder to the other half of the batter.

Add alternating scoops of the two batters to the prepared pan. Using a butter knife, swirl the batters together, without combining them fully.

Bake the cake until a toothpick inserted into the center comes out clean, 60 to 65 minutes. Transfer the pan to a rack to cool slightly, then remove the cake from the pan, transfer it to the rack, and let it cool completely before slicing.

The cake can be stored in an airtight container at room temperature for up to 1 week or, well wrapped, in the freezer for up to 1 month. Thaw at room temperature before serving.

Stay away from glass loaf pans, as they hold on to heat and can cause the edges of your cake to brown too quickly or burn. Reserve glass pans for pies.

Malted Chocolate Cream Pie

This decadent pie uses six egg yolks in the filling to ensure the richest cream pie ever. If you're feeling lazy, you could skip the crust and the whipped cream and serve the filling as pudding.

CRUST

Flour for rolling

1 recipe Laminated Butter Pie Pastry (page 5)

FILLING

¾ cup (105 grams) bittersweet chocolate, chopped

¾ cup (105 grams) milk chocolate, chopped

¼ cup (50 grams) granulated sugar

2 tablespoons (16 grams) cornstarch

½ teaspoon kosher salt

½ cup (72 grams) malted milk powder

6 large (120 grams) egg yolks

3 cups (720 grams) whole milk

2 tablespoons (¼ stick; 28 grams) butter, softened

1½ teaspoons pure vanilla extract

TOPPING

¾ cup (180 grams) cold heavy cream

A mix of milk and dark chocolate makes the filling more chocolatey than one made with all milk chocolate and lighter than one that uses all dark chocolate: a happy medium. They both contribute sweetness and creaminess to the filling.

Malt powder is made from a sprouted grain, usually barley, that is dried, ground, and mixed with wheat flour. Malted milk powder is made by adding powdered milk to malt powder.

PREPARE THE CRUST. On a lightly floured surface, roll the pastry out to a ¼- to ⅛-inch-thick circle. Fit it into a 9-inch pie plate. Trim the edges so that you have a ½-inch (or a tiny bit more) overhang. Fold the edges over and crimp the edges. Freeze the crust for 20 minutes.

Preheat the oven to 375°F.

Set the frozen shell on a rimmed baking sheet and prick the bottom a few times with a fork. Set a piece of parchment paper in the pie shell and fill it to the brim with pie weights, dried beans, or rice.

Bake until the pastry under the parchment is set and light golden brown, about 25 minutes (carefully lift up the parchment to check). Remove from the oven and remove the parchment and weights, then return the shell to the oven. Bake until the shell is evenly golden brown and dry, about 10 more minutes. Remove from the oven and set aside to cool completely.

PREPARE THE FILLING. Place the bittersweet and milk chocolate in a medium bowl and set a fine-mesh sieve over the bowl.

In a medium saucepan, whisk together the sugar, cornstarch, salt, malted milk powder, egg yolks, milk, and butter. Heat the mixture over medium heat, stirring constantly, until it has come to a very slow boil and boil gently, whisking or stirring for 1 minute, or until it has thickened nicely. You may have to switch between a whisk and a spatula to ensure a smooth texture.

Immediately pour the custard through the sieve onto the chocolate, using a rubber spatula to push the custard through the sieve; discard any solids in the sieve. Whisk the hot custard into the chocolate until the mixture is smooth. Stir in the vanilla.

Pour the custard into the baked crust, cover loosely with plastic, and refrigerate until completely chilled, about 6 hours.

Whip the cream to medium-soft peaks. Top the pie with the whipped cream to serve. Store leftovers up to 3 days in the fridge.

Cinnamon-and-Cardamom–Spiced Churros

MAKES ABOUT 12 CHURROS

These churros are made with a slightly modified version of pâte à choux dough. Dip them in melted chocolate, Crème Anglaise (page 97), or your morning coffee.

6 tablespoons (¾ stick; 85 grams) butter

2 teaspoons granulated sugar

½ teaspoon kosher salt

¾ cup (180 grams) water

¾ cup (102 grams) all-purpose flour

2 large (100 grams) eggs

Neutral oil for deep-frying

TO FINISH

½ cup (100 grams) granulated sugar

1½ teaspoons ground cinnamon

½ teaspoon ground cardamom

In a medium saucepan, combine the butter, sugar, salt, and water and bring to a simmer over medium heat, stirring with a wooden spoon. As soon as the mixture comes to a simmer, add the flour and stir until the dough forms a ball and pulls away from the sides of the pan, about 1 minute. Remove the pan from the heat and let the dough cool for 3 to 4 minutes, stirring occasionally.

One at a time, add the eggs to the dough, stirring vigorously after each addition with the wooden spoon. The dough will break apart and slide around in the pan and then come back together.

Fit a piping bag with a ¼-inch open star tip and transfer the dough to the bag.

In a large pot fitted with a candy thermometer, heat the oil to 350°F. Line a large plate with paper towels. In a small bowl,

combine the sugar, cinnamon, and cardamom.

Once the oil has reached the correct temperature, pipe 6- to 7-inch lengths of dough directly into the hot oil, cutting them apart with a pair of scissors as you go. Fry the churros in batches of 3 until slightly puffed and golden brown, 3 to 4 minutes, flipping them halfway through. Transfer the fried churros to the lined plate to drain for a few minutes, then toss the warm churros in the sugar mixture. Repeat with the remaining dough and sugar. Serve immediately.

Don't worry if you don't have a star tip. For a slightly more rustic star tip, reinforce one corner of a resealable plastic bag with several layers of Scotch tape to make it stiff. Then carefully cut what looks like a crown out of the reinforced corner. This works for piping simple frosting designs too.

Maple Ginger Pots de Crème

SERVES 6

This custard is thickened with egg yolks alone. Without cornstarch, the custard is more susceptible to curdling, but using a water bath ensures that it cooks slowly and gently, for an ethereal texture. Sour cream plays well with ginger, contributing a welcome tang and even more creaminess to the dessert.

¾ cup (312 grams) dark maple syrup

1½ cups (360 grams) heavy cream

1 cup (240 grams) whole milk

½ teaspoon kosher salt

½ vanilla bean, split lengthwise in half

Two 2-inch-wide slices fresh ginger (unpeeled is fine!)

6 large (120 grams) egg yolks, beaten well

Boiling water for the water bath

Sour cream for serving

In a medium saucepan, bring the maple syrup to a simmer over medium-high heat (reserving the measuring cup you used). Maintaining a gentle simmer, cook the syrup until it has reduced to ½ cup, about 8 minutes. Pour the syrup back into the measuring cup to check, but be careful! It will be very hot. Set it aside to cool.

In the same pan, combine the cream, milk, salt, and vanilla bean and bring the mixture just to a bare simmer. Immediately turn off the heat, add the ginger, and cover the pan. (You don't want to simmer the cream and milk with the ginger, as the acidity of the ginger could encourage the eggs to curdle.) Set aside to cool and infuse for at least 30 minutes, and up to 2 hours.

Preheat the oven to 325°F. Set six 6-ounce teacups or ramekins in a baking dish.

Add the egg yolks and reduced maple syrup to the cream mixture and whisk to combine. Strain the mixture through a fine-mesh sieve into a large glass measuring cup.

Divide the mixture evenly among the cups. Set the baking dish in the oven and carefully add enough boiling water to the dish to come halfway up the sides of the cups. Cover the dish with foil.

Bake until the custards are just set but still have a bit of jiggle in the center, 30 to 35 minutes. Remove the baking dish from the oven, uncover, and let the custards come to room temperature in the water, then remove them from the water bath, cover with plastic wrap, and refrigerate for at least 2 hours before serving. (You can make these up to 24 hours in advance.)

Top the pots de crème with sour cream to serve.

The goal is to reduce the maple syrup to remove water and concentrate the flavor. Go slowly so that the syrup doesn't scald or turn into candy.

Test for doneness with a thermometer if you're at all unsure. The custards should be 150°F to 155°F. The hole in the custard you test should close up as the custard cools, but if not, simply cover it up with sour cream.

Pistachio and Chocolate Eclairs

MAKES 12 ÉCLAIRS

Unlike the crémeux for the Chocolate Crémeux Slice (page 22), this one is made with gelatin as well as egg yolks, giving it the texture of a silky mousse. Without the melted chocolate, which helps firm up the custard as it cools, this crémeux needs a bit more help with structure.

I like to use semisweet or even milk chocolate for the glaze so as not to overpower the delicate pistachio flavor of the filling.

CRÉMEUX

- 1 cup (140 grams) raw pistachios, plus more chopped for garnish
- ¼ cup (50 grams) granulated sugar
- 1 cup (240 grams) heavy cream
- ¾ cup (180 grams) whole milk
- 1 tablespoon (15 grams) cold water
- ½ teaspoon unflavored gelatin
- 4 large (80 grams) egg yolks
- ¾ teaspoon kosher salt

PUFFS

- 6 tablespoons (¾ stick; 85 grams) butter
- 2 teaspoons granulated sugar
- ½ teaspoon kosher salt
- ¾ cup (180 grams) water
- ¾ cup (102 grams) all-purpose flour
- 3 large (150 grams) eggs

GLAZE

- ½ cup (120 grams) heavy cream
- ½ teaspoon kosher salt
- 1¼ cups (175 grams) milk or semisweet chocolate, chopped
- 1 tablespoon (21 grams) corn syrup

Corn syrup gives the glaze shine and flow, but it's not essential if you'd rather not use it.

If you use a high-speed blender, like a Vitamix, the nuts will be fine enough to leave them in the custard.

PREPARE THE CRÉMEUX. Combine the pistachios and sugar in a food processor or high-speed blender and finely grind the nuts.

In a small saucepan, whisk together ¾ cup of the heavy cream, the milk, and ground pistachio mixture and bring to a boil over medium heat. Remove from the heat, cover, and let stand for 30 minutes.

Pour the cold water into a small bowl and sprinkle the gelatin evenly over the top. Let stand for 5 minutes.

Add the egg yolks and salt to the pistachio mixture and cook over medium heat, stirring with a wooden spoon, until the custard has thickened slightly, about 4 minutes. You should be able to draw a clear line with your finger through the custard on the back of the wooden spoon. (The custard should read 170°F on an instant-read thermometer.) Remove from the heat and stir in the dissolved gelatin.

Pour the custard through a fine-mesh sieve set over a bowl, pressing on the solids to extract as much custard as possible. (Don't discard those pistachio solids! Spread the paste on a slice of buttered brioche. Mm.) Cover the custard with plastic wrap pressed directly against the surface and chill until cold.

Using an immersion blender, blend the crémeux for 1 to 2 minutes, until creamy and smooth. (You can also do this in a regular blender, then return the crémeux to the bowl.) You should have about 1¾ cups crémeux. Cover with plastic wrap and refrigerate again until chilled.

continues

PREPARE THE PUFFS. In a medium saucepan, combine the butter, sugar, salt, and water and bring to a simmer over medium heat, stirring with a wooden spoon. As soon as the mixture comes to a simmer, add the flour, stirring constantly, and then stir until the dough forms a ball and pulls away from the sides of the pan, about 1 minute. Remove the pan from the heat and let the dough cool for 3 to 4 minutes, stirring occasionally.

Preheat the oven to 400°F.

One at a time, add the eggs to the dough, stirring vigorously with the wooden spoon after each addition. The dough will break apart and slide around in the pan and then come back together.

Transfer the dough to a piping bag fitted with a ¾- to 1-inch plain tip. Line two baking sheets with parchment paper.

Pipe the dough into 4½ x ¾-inch lengths about 3 inches apart on the prepared baking sheets. With a damp fingertip, flatten any points. (You can also freeze the unbaked piped éclairs on the baking sheets. Once they are frozen solid, transfer them to an airtight container. Bake them from frozen, adding a few minutes as necessary.)

Bake the éclairs until they are deep golden brown, puffed, and crisp, about 30 minutes, rotating the sheets halfway through. Remove the éclairs from the oven and turn the oven off.

Poke either end of each éclair with a toothpick to allow some steam to escape. Return the puffs to the oven and prop the door open a crack with a wooden spoon. Allow the puffs to dry out in the oven for about 15 minutes, then transfer the baking sheets to racks to cool completely.

PREPARE THE GLAZE. In a small saucepan, combine the cream and salt and bring to a simmer over medium heat. Remove from the heat and stir in the chocolate and corn syrup. Let the mixture stand for 1 minute, then whisk until smooth.

ASSEMBLE THE ÉCLAIRS. In a small bowl, whip the remaining ¼ cup cream to stiff peaks. Fold the whipped cream into the pistachio crémeux and transfer the crémeux to a pastry bag fitted with a fluted tip.

Slice the top third off each éclair and set aside. Fill the bases of the éclairs with the crémeux. Dip the tops of the éclairs in the glaze and set them on top of the filled bases. Sprinkle with chopped pistachios. Serve immediately.

Saffron and Cardamom Crème Caramel

SERVES 8

Saffron, the stigmas of a type of crocus, is the most expensive spice there is by weight. Fitting for a dessert that looks like a beautiful bar of gold.

1 cup (240 grams) whole milk

1 cup (240 grams) heavy cream

¼ teaspoon saffron threads

10 cardamom pods (2 grams), slightly smashed

2 tablespoons (30 grams) water

¾ cup (150 grams) granulated sugar, plus ⅓ cup (67 grams)

2 large (100 grams) eggs

4 large (80 grams) egg yolks

1 12-ounce can evaporated milk

Boiling water for the water bath

In a medium saucepan, combine the milk, cream, saffron, and cardamom and bring to a simmer over medium heat. Immediately turn off the heat, cover, and let stand for at least 30 minutes, and up to 2 hours.

Have ready a 4½ x 8½-inch loaf pan. Add the water to a small saucepan, then pour the ¾ cup sugar into the center of the pan. Bring the mixture to simmer over medium-high heat; do not stir. Once the caramel starts to turn amber in spots, after about 4 minutes, carefully swirl the pan. Then continue to cook, swirling the pan often, until the caramel is evenly deep amber, about 6 minutes. Keep a close eye on the pan; once the caramel starts to color, it can burn very quickly.

Immediately pour the caramel into the loaf pan. Very carefully swirl the caramel to coat the bottom and sides evenly (the caramel will be very hot!). Set aside to cool completely.

Preheat the oven to 325°F.

Add the eggs, egg yolks, evaporated milk, and the remaining ⅓ cup sugar to the steeped milk mixture and mix well. Strain the mixture through a fine-mesh sieve into the caramel-lined loaf pan. Set the loaf pan in a baking dish.

Set the baking dish in the oven, then carefully pour enough boiling water into the dish to come halfway up the sides of the loaf pan. Cover with foil.

Bake until the custard is just set but still has a bit of jiggle in the center, 60 to 75 minutes. Remove the dish from the oven, uncover, and let the custard cool to room temperature in the water bath. Then remove the pan from the water, cover with plastic wrap, and refrigerate for at least 4 hours, or up to 24 hours, before serving.

To serve, use a sharp knife to release the custard from the sides of the pan. Carefully flip the custard out onto a serving plate; there will be a lot of liquid caramel, so choose your plate accordingly! You don't want to lose any of it. It's too good.

Store leftovers, well wrapped, in the fridge for up to 3 days.

A loaf pan makes one big crème caramel that's easy to transport and to serve at a party.

When making the caramel, always add the water to the pan first, then add the sugar to the center of the pan. This helps keep sugar crystals off the sides of the pan, where they could fall back into the sugar syrup and cause crystallization. See page 49 for a caramel cooking refresher.

Coconut Pandan Rice Pudding

SERVES 4

Pandan, or screwpine, is a common flavoring in South and Southeastern Asia and one of my all-time favorites. It's sweet and floral like vanilla but slightly more vegetal, in the loveliest way. It grew all over my grandmother's garden in Sri Lanka, and every time we visited, my brother would cut and dry plenty to take home. I've been throwing it into puddings, cakes, and cocktails ever since. Look for it fresh or frozen at Asian markets.

Most of the creaminess in this pudding comes from the starch in the Arborio rice and the whole milk, but a couple of golden egg yolks added at the end transform the pudding into something both silky and rich.

2 cups (480 grams) whole milk

½ cup (90 grams) Arborio rice

⅓ cup (66 grams) packed dark brown sugar or jaggery

Pinch of kosher salt

2 pandan leaves (about 10 grams)

2 large (40 grams) egg yolks

1½ teaspoons pure vanilla extract

1 13.5-ounce can full-fat coconut milk (1¾ cups)

Canned coconut milk varies in quality and flavor. Taste several brands before making one your go-to.

Jaggery is a type of sugar made from the sap of coconut or date palms.

In a medium pot, combine the milk, rice, sugar, salt, and pandan leaves, bring to a low simmer over medium heat, and cook, stirring often, until the milk has reduced and thickened and the rice is soft, about 20 minutes. Remove from the heat.

In a small bowl, whisk the egg yolks together with a few spoonfuls of the hot pudding. Add about 1 cup more pudding, little by little. Then add the yolk mixture back to the pot, along with the coconut milk.

Return the pot to medium-low heat and cook, stirring, until bubbles start to break the surface, about 3 minutes, and then cook it for an additional minute. Stir in the vanilla extract. Transfer the pudding to a serving bowl, remove the pandan, cover, and chill until cold before serving.

Store leftovers in an airtight container in the fridge for up to 3 days.

When adding egg yolks to cornstarch-thickened puddings and custards, you must cook them long enough to kill their alpha-amylase enzyme; otherwise it will deactivate the cornstarch.

If the pudding firms up too much as it chills, simply stir in a bit of milk before you serve it. If you like, stir some Bittersweet Caramel Sauce (page 52) into the pudding just before serving.

pandan leaves

Coffee Crème Croissant Bread Pudding

SERVES 8 TO 10

Hang around your favorite bakery around closing time and see if you can snag a couple of older croissants at a discount before they hit the compost. Stale bread will absorb the coffee-flavored custard more readily. Drizzle the pudding with Crème Anglaise (page 97), Bittersweet Caramel Sauce (page 52), or both!

Butter for the baking dish

2 teaspoons pure vanilla extract

2 teaspoons espresso powder

3 large (150 grams) eggs

4 large (80 grams) egg yolks

1 cup (240 grams) heavy cream

¾ cup (230 grams) sweetened condensed milk

2½ cups (600 grams) whole milk

¾ teaspoon kosher salt

4 or 5 day-old croissants (about 390 grams), sliced

Sanding sugar for sprinkling

Boiling water for the water bath

Confectioners' sugar for dusting (optional)

> Swap the croissants for any soft enriched bread like challah or brioche, but avoid anything too crusty or sour.

Preheat the oven to 350°F. Butter a 9-inch square baking dish.

In a large bowl, combine the vanilla and espresso powder. Let stand for a minute or two, until the espresso granules are dissolved.

Add the eggs and egg yolks and beat until completely combined. Whisk in the cream, condensed milk, whole milk, and salt.

Arrange the sliced croissants in the prepared baking dish, overlapping to fit, and pour the egg mixture over them. Press down gently on the croissants with a spatula to make sure all the slices are immersed and will soak up the liquid. Let stand at room temperature for 10 minutes.

Sprinkle the top of the bread pudding evenly with sanding sugar. Cover the baking dish tightly with aluminum foil and set it in a large roasting pan. Pour enough boiling water into the roasting pan to come about halfway up the sides of the baking dish.

Bake until the center of the custard is almost set but still slightly wet, about 25 minutes. Carefully remove the pan from the oven and remove the foil, then return the pan to the oven and bake until the custard is set in the center and the top is golden, about 30 minutes longer. It's shockingly easy to misjudge the timing on a bread pudding; it often looks puffed and browned before the custard in the center has set. So even if you think yours is done, dig around in the center and make sure you don't see any liquid before you pull it from the oven. Any little holes you've created can be covered up with a light dusting of confectioners' sugar if necessary. Carefully remove the pan from the oven and let the pudding cool in the water bath for about 20 minutes.

Serve the pudding warm, or cover and chill to serve cold. It can be stored in the fridge for up to 5 days.

> The water bath keeps the temperature of the custard mixture from rising too quickly, preventing it from curdling and helping to ensure the perfect texture.

Coconut Lime Layer Cake

SERVES 8 TO 10

Tart lime curd nestled between layers of sweet and tender coconut cake hits all the right notes.

CAKE

- 10 tablespoons (1¼ sticks; 141 grams) butter, at room temperature, plus more for the baking sheet
- 2 cups (240 grams) cake flour
- 1 tablespoon (12 grams) baking powder
- 1¼ cups (250 grams) granulated sugar
- 4 large eggs (200 grams), separated, at room temperature
- 2 teaspoons pure vanilla extract
- ¾ cup (180 grams) whole milk, at room temperature
- 1 cup (70 grams) toasted unsweetened shredded coconut

FILLING

- 1 recipe Lime Curd (page 95) or store-bought lime or lemon curd

FROSTING

- 8 ounces (226 grams) cream cheese, very soft
- 8 tablespoons (1 stick; 113 grams) butter, at room temperature
- 1 cup (120 grams) confectioners' sugar
- 1½ teaspoons pure vanilla extract

- 1½ cups (105 grams) toasted unsweetened shredded coconut

To toast coconut, spread it evenly on a light-colored baking sheet and bake in a 350°F oven until golden, stirring often, 5 to 10 minutes.

PREPARE THE CAKE. Preheat the oven to 350°F. Butter a 13 x 18-inch rimmed baking sheet.

In a medium bowl, whisk together the cake flour and baking powder.

In a large bowl, with an electric mixer on medium speed, beat together the butter and 1 cup of the sugar until fluffy, about 3 minutes. Beat in the egg yolks and vanilla. Beat in half of the flour mixture, then all of the milk, and then the remaining flour mixture. Do not overmix. Fold in the coconut.

In a large clean bowl, with clean beaters, beat the egg whites on medium-high until they are foamy and the yellowish tinge has disappeared. With the mixer on high speed , add the remaining ¼ cup sugar a little at a time, and continue beating until stiff peaks form, about 4 minutes.

Stir a spoonful of the beaten egg whites into the batter to loosen it, and then, with a balloon whisk, fold in the rest of the whites. Tip the batter into the prepared baking sheet and carefully spread it into an even

layer. (Be careful not to overwork the batter, so that you don't lose all the air.)

Bake the cake until it is golden brown and springs back when gently pressed in the center, about 20 minutes. Transfer to a rack to cool for 15 minutes, then flip the cake out onto a rack to cool completely.

Slice the cake into four 13 x 4½-inch rectangles. Set one piece on a serving plate and top with a third of the lime curd, spreading it evenly. Repeat two more times with two more cake layers and the remaining lime curd, then place the remaining piece of cake on top. Cover and chill for at least 1 hour, and up to 24 hours.

PREPARE THE FROSTING. In a large bowl, with an electic mixer on medium, beat together the cream cheese, butter, confectioners' sugar, and vanilla until smooth.

Spread the frosting evenly over the top and sides of the cake. Press the coconut evenly into the frosting. Refrigerate, covered, until bringing to room temperature for about 30 minutes before serving.

Store leftovers, well wrapped, in the fridge, but let the slices warm up at room temperature before serving.

No cake pans required for this three-layered beauty! The layers are baked all at once in a rimmed baking sheet. Easy peasy.

Cream Cheese Ice Cream with Dates

Thanks to a generous dose of cream cheese and a lot of egg yolks, this custard-based ice cream has the texture of the most decadent soft-serve you've ever eaten. It needs no garnish, but if you're feeling fancy, you can serve it topped with some warm almond or peanut butter and flaky salt.

8 large (160 grams) egg yolks

1 cup (200 grams) granulated sugar

Pinch of kosher salt

2 cups (480 grams) heavy cream

8 ounces (226 grams) cream cheese, cut into pieces, at room temperature

1 vanilla bean, split lengthwise and seeds scraped out, seeds and bean reserved

1½ cups (300 grams) finely chopped Medjool dates, frozen until firm

Use super-soft Medjool dates here. When frozen, they will become chewy, not hard.

In a large saucepan, whisk together the egg yolks, sugar, and salt until pale yellow. Whisking constantly, slowly add the cream, cream cheese, and vanilla bean and seeds. Heat the mixture over medium-low heat, stirring constantly with a wooden spoon, until it is thick enough to coat the back of the spoon, 10 to 12 minutes; it should register about 170°F on an instant-read thermometer.

Strain the mixture through a fine-mesh sieve set over a bowl. Discard any solids left in the sieve. Cool to room temperature, then cover with plastic wrap and refrigerate for at least 4 hours, and up to overnight.

Set a 9 x 5-inch loaf pan in the freezer to chill. Churn the ice cream mixture in an ice cream machine according to the manufacturer's instructions. During the last few minutes of processing, add the dates.

Transfer the ice cream to the prepared loaf pan, cover well with plastic wrap, and freeze until firm. The ice cream can be stored, well wrapped, in the freezer for up to 2 weeks.

The cream cheese makes the mixture very thick, so it's a good idea to check the temperature with an instant-read thermometer to ensure that the eggs are properly cooked.

Fresh Kiwi and Vanilla Bean Cake en Croûte

I find that it's hard to capture kiwi's subtle flavor in baked goods. So, instead of putting them in the batter, I cover the top of the cake with slices of the fruit before baking. That way, with every bite, you get a floral kiwi pop first, followed by fluffy cake and crisp, buttery pastry. Instead of kiwis, you can try any somewhat dry fruit, like apples or crisp pears.

"En croûte" means in a pastry crust in French. Baking a fruity cake in a pastry shell isn't traditional as far as I know, but it should be.

PASTRY

Flour, for the work surface

1 recipe Rough Puff Pastry (page 7)

CAKE

½ cup (100 grams) granulated sugar

½ vanilla bean, split lengthwise and seeds scraped out and reserved

2 large (100 grams) eggs

¼ cup (60 grams) whole milk

2 tablespoons (¼ stick; 28 grams) butter, melted and cooled slightly

Pinch of kosher salt

¾ cup (102 grams) all-purpose flour

1 teaspoon baking powder

4 kiwis, peeled and sliced into thin rounds (420 grams)

TO FINISH

Strained apricot jam

Apricot jam adds gloss as well sweetness.

PREPARE THE PASTRY. On a lightly floured surface, roll the pastry dough out to about a 9 x 11-inch rectangle (it will be between ⅛ and ¼ inch thick). Trim the edges. Using a sharp knife, score a 1-inch border all around the edges; don't cut all the way through the dough. (This will result in a risen border to enclose the batter.) Dock the pastry within the border all over with a fork. Transfer to a baking sheet and freeze for 15 minutes.

Preheat the oven to 425°F.

Set the pastry shell on a parchment-lined rimmed baking sheet and bake until puffed and golden, about 20 minutes.

MEANWHILE, PREPARE THE CAKE. In a medium bowl, rub the sugar and vanilla seeds together with your fingers. Then whisk in the eggs, milk, butter, and salt. Fold in the flour and baking powder.

Remove the tart shell from the oven. Using a spoon, gently tap down the center, within the border. Spread the cake batter evenly over the pastry within the border. Arrange the kiwi slices on top.

Bake the cake until it is golden brown and set in the center, about 25 minutes. Press it gently in the center with your finger to check. Remove from the oven and brush with the apricot jam while it is still warm. Serve warm or at room temperature.

This tart is best the day it's made.

Docking pastry, or pricking it with a fork, makes tiny holes that allow the steam created in the oven to escape. Here it keeps the dough in the center from puffing too much.

For a less rustic-looking tart, you can bake this in a fluted tart pan with a removable bottom. Either way works great.

Depending on how high the pastry edges rise, it's possible that a bit of the cake batter may overflow. Don't worry! That's what the lined rimmed baking sheet is for.

Peanut Butter and Chocolate Snack Cake

MAKES 16 BARS

If you call a cake a "snack cake," it means you can eat it at any time of day! The two eggs in the batter give this cake a tender, fluffy texture. For a chewier, blondie-like texture, just use one egg.

CAKE

- 10 tablespoons (1¼ sticks; 141 grams) butter, plus more for the pan
- ¾ cup (150 grams) packed light or dark brown sugar
- ½ cup (115 grams) creamy peanut butter (not natural)
- 2 large (100 grams) eggs
- 1½ teaspoons pure vanilla extract
- 1 cup (136 grams) all-purpose flour
- ½ teaspoon baking powder
- ¼ teaspoon baking soda
- ¾ teaspoon kosher salt
- 1 cup (140 grams) bittersweet chocolate, chopped

FROSTING

- 2 tablespoons (11 grams) natural or Dutch-processed cocoa powder
- ¼ cup (60 grams) boiling water
- ½ cup (70 grams) good-quality milk chocolate, melted
- Pinch of kosher salt
- 8 tablespoons (1 stick; 113 grams) butter, at room temperature

I love natural peanut butter for snacking, but in most cases, conventional peanut butter, with its added sugar and homogenized texture, is better for baking.

You can use whichever type of cocoa powder you prefer in the frosting, but make certain that it is unsweetened. Paired with milk chocolate, unsweetened cocoa creates a balanced chocolate flavor.

PREPARE THE CAKE. Preheat the oven to 350°F. Butter a 9-inch square baking pan and line it with parchment paper, leaving a 2-inch overhang on two opposite sides.

In a medium saucepan, combine the butter and sugar and heat over medium until the butter is melted. Remove from the heat and whisk vigorously until well combined. Let cool slightly.

Once the butter mixture has cooled a bit, whisk in the peanut butter, then whisk in the eggs one a time. Whisk in the vanilla. Add the flour, baking powder, baking soda, and salt and stir to combine. Stir in the chocolate. (Some of the chocolate will melt a bit, which will gives the baked cake a pleasant marbled effect.) Transfer the batter to the prepared pan and smooth the top.

Bake until the top of the cake looks just set and a toothpick inserted into the center comes out with a few moist crumbs attached, 18 to 20 minutes. Do not overbake. Transfer to a rack and let the cake cool completely in the pan.

PREPARE THE FROSTING. In a large bowl, whisk together the cocoa powder and boiling water until smooth. Remove from the heat and let cool.

Whisk the melted chocolate and salt into the cocoa mixture. Add the butter and beat with an electric mixer on medium speed until smooth and fluffy.

Spread the frosting over the top of the cooled cake.

To serve, use the paper overhang to transfer the cake from the pan to a cutting board. Cut into 16 bars.

The cake bars can be stored in an airtight container at room temperature for up to 3 days. The unfrosted cake can be stored in the freezer for up to 1 month. Thaw at room temperature and then frost if desired.

Chocolate Mint Sandwich Cookies

MAKES ABOUT 18 SANDWICH COOKIES

Although these cookies are in the egg chapter, there are no eggs in the recipe. I've included these here to demonstrate what eggs do in cookie doughs and how different the texture is without them. Eggs act as a binder in the dough, giving the finished cookies structure and chew. Without eggs, these cookies are crumbly like shortbread and super-tender.

I like to eat these frozen. The mint tastes even more refreshing when the cookies are cold.

COOKIES

- 1½ cups (204 grams) all-purpose flour, plus more for rolling
- ½ cup (43 grams) Dutch-processed cocoa powder, sifted
- ½ teaspoon baking powder
- ½ teaspoon baking soda
- ½ teaspoon kosher salt
- 12 tablespoons (1½ sticks; 170 grams) butter, at room temperature
- ½ cup (100 grams) packed dark brown sugar
- ¼ cup (50 grams) granulated sugar

FILLING

- 2 cups (240 grams) confectioners' sugar
- ¼ cup (60 grams) heavy cream
- 3 tablespoons (⅜ stick; 42 grams) butter, at room temperature
- ¼ teaspoon peppermint extract

Don't worry about sifting the sugar here. You can't see the cream in the cookies, so who cares if it has a few tiny lumps?

Use black cocoa, which is ultra-Dutch processed cocoa powder, to make the darkest and chocolatiest version of these cookies.

Swap out the peppermint extract for another flavor if mint isn't your thing.

PREPARE THE COOKIES. In a small bowl, whisk together the flour, cocoa, baking powder, baking soda, and salt.

In a medium bowl, with an electric mixer on medium speed, beat together the butter, brown sugar, and granulated sugar until creamy, 1 to 2 minutes. Add the flour mixture and beat to combine.

Tip the dough out, divide it in half, and flatten each half into a disk. Wrap in plastic wrap and chill for at least 1 hour and up to 3 days. You can also freeze the dough for up to 1 month.

Preheat the oven to 350°F, with the racks in the upper and lower thirds of the oven. Line two rimmed baking sheets with parchment paper. Let the dough stand at room temperature for about 5 minutes.

On a lightly floured sheet of parchment, roll one disk of dough out to about ⅛ inch thick. Using a 2-inch round fluted cookie cutter, cut out cookies and transfer them to the prepared sheets. You can reroll the scraps once.

Bake the cookies until they are set and dry, about 8 minutes, rotating the sheets halfway through. Let the cookies cool completely on the sheets on racks. (They will be delicate until they cool.)

PREPARE THE FILLING. In a large bowl, stir together the confectioners' sugar, heavy cream, butter, and peppermint extract with a wooden spoon. (You will have about 1 cup filling.)

Flip half of the cookies over. Top each one with about 1 tablespoon filling, then cover with another cookie, flat side down, and press down gently to spread the filling.

The cookies can be stored in an airtight container at room temperature for up to 3 days or in the freezer for 1 month.

If you roll out the dough on a piece of parchment, if it ever gets too warm, you can use the parchment to transfer it to the fridge to firm up a bit.

Flours,
Nuts & Cocoa

Imagine that baking a cake is like building a house. The butter, sugar, and eggs work the way the cement and nails do: they hold the house together. But in order to construct that house, you need some bricks. The bricks of the cake are flour, nuts, and/or cocoa, sometimes used together and sometimes in place of one another. Most baking recipes include at least one of these ingredients to add structure and bulk, as well as flavor.

Flour Basics

Flour gives baked goods structure and texture. It helps distribute the liquid and fats in batters evenly. It helps keep doughs from sticking to your work surface and rolling pins. It thickens pie fillings. The list goes on and on. But when it comes to flour, I think the most important lesson to learn is how to measure it. I tell everyone to invest in an inexpensive little kitchen scale. Not only does it ensure accurate measurements, but it's also a much neater way of measuring. Imagine just adding all of your dry ingredients to one bowl instead of using multiple cups and spoons. But good old cup measures, if you use them properly, are just fine for these recipes too. And, when the amount is small, I still recommend sticking to measuring spoons. It's hard to get an accurate measurement for anything under a tablespoon with a standard kitchen scale.

Scoop and sweep for the win.

To measure flour with a dry measuring cup (don't use a liquid measuring cup), scoop the flour into the cup with a spoon or something similar. Then level it off with a bench scraper or the back of a knife. Don't use the measuring cup as a scoop, and don't pack the flour into it. If you bake often, I highly recommend transferring your flour into a wide-mouth bin and leaving the bench scraper in there. The scraper can then be both your scooper and sweeper. Try it. You'll never go back.

"Don't overmix"—what's that about?

In plain dry wheat flour, the protein strands are free and loose. Add some water to that flour, though, and work it a bit, and the protein strands combine and strengthen to form gluten. This is necessary to add structure to batters and doughs, which allows them to trap gas (from the leavener) and air (from creaming the butter and sugar or from steam—see more on that in the Butter chapter) and thus rise. But if you overmix, too much gluten can develop and make baked goods tough. When we add fat to that flour the protein strands become coated and therefore less likely to absorb water or to bond and strengthen. That's why we usually add the flour mixture to creamed butter before adding liquid. Fat makes baked goods tender. In the case of enriched bread, where we actually want a nice chewy texture to develop, we knead the dough a bit to build up gluten and then add the fat.

Forget About Sifting Flour . . . But Do Whisk Well

These days, sifting all-purpose flour is unnecessary. But do use a whisk to combine the dry ingredients thoroughly before incorporating them into the rest of a dough or batter. Making sure that the leavener (or leaveners) is evenly dispersed is important for creating evenly risen cakes and cookies.

In some cases, when the recipe is for a simple bar or cookie and the amounts are small, I call for adding the dry ingredients directly to the batter. When it simplifies the recipe and makes for fewer dirty bowls, I'm all for doing it this way. But if you notice that your baking soda or baking powder is older and has a few lumps, then whisk it with the flour first to be safe.

My Favorite Flours

Keep in mind that the type of flour called for in a recipe will yield a specific result. Flours are not always interchangeable.

ALL-PURPOSE FLOUR: This is made from a blend of hard and soft wheat, and it's suitable for the widest array of baked goods. I buy King Arthur Unbleached All-Purpose Flour, and that's what I used for all of the recipes in this book. Some say that bleached flour is better for more delicate pastries and that unbleached should be used for yeasted doughs. I find the difference to be negligible, so you can use whatever kind you have.

WHOLE WHEAT FLOUR: Whole wheat flour is milled from whole wheatberries, including both the bran and the germ. It's slightly coarser than all-purpose flour. If you want to use it in your favorite recipes, start by subbing in 25 percent of the all-purpose flour with whole wheat.

BREAD FLOUR: Bread flour is made from hard wheat with a higher protein content than the wheat used for all-purpose and whole wheat flours. If you use a strong unbleached all-purpose flour like King Arthur brand, you can swap it in for bread flour, but you won't get the same chewiness.

CAKE FLOUR: Cake flour is a low-protein flour that's made from soft wheat and has been chlorinated. It does tend to clump, so give it a good whisk before measuring it. In a pinch, you can substitute in all-purpose flour for cake flour, using the following proportions: For every cup of cake flour, use ¾ cup plus 2 tablespoons all-purpose flour, and add 2 tablespoons cornstarch.

BUCKWHEAT FLOUR: Buckwheat is not actually a type of wheat. The flour is made by roasting and milling buckwheat seeds, which are related to sorrel and rhubarb. The flavor is strong, nutty, and somewhat tart. I like it best blended with some all-purpose flour.

NUT FLOUR: Nut flours are made from finely milled nuts. As far as I can tell, there is no distinction between nut flour and nut meal, although different brands use different terms. You can find some of these flours made with (unblanched) or without (blanched) the skins, and I think they are interchangeable in terms of flavor. You can make nut flours yourself in a food processor or a high-speed blender, the former making slightly coarser flour than the latter.

RYE FLOUR: You can find dark rye, medium rye, and light rye if you look hard enough. Light rye has had the germ and bran removed. Medium rye has more bran. Most dark rye will contain whole rye kernels.

Any of these will work for the recipes in this book, you just have to decide how pronounced you'd like the rye flavor to be.

If you have the space, it's a great idea to store all flours in airtight containers in the fridge. Whole wheat and other whole grain flours are especially likely to go rancid at room temperature because of the fat from the germ, but all flour can turn eventually. Before using it, give your flour a good sniff. It should smell slightly sweet but otherwise fairly neutral. If you smell anything off, compost or toss your flour and buy a fresh bag.

Nut Basics

Not only do nuts add flavor and texture to baked goods, they're also high in protein and rich in vitamins. Most nuts are quite oily, which is wonderful for baking but makes them susceptible to spoiling. If you have space, keep your nuts in the freezer. I store them alongside bottles of Chablis in my wine fridge, as even a few degrees cooler than room temperature will keep them fresher for longer. Give nuts a good whiff or even a quick taste before you add them to any recipe. You'll know they're rancid if they have an off odor or unpleasant flavor. In the past, I've bought nuts from the supermarket only to find at home that they are rancid. Even if you think they're fresh, taste them to make sure. Rancid nuts can really ruin a cookie.

Toasting

Toasting nuts can tame any bitterness or astringency and bring out their flavor, but not every nut needs to be toasted. It depends on the kind of nut and how you'll be using it. Walnuts, for example, become sweeter when toasted and take on a pleasant roasted flavor, but the delicate flavor of fresh pistachios is muted by toasting.

To toast nuts, spread them out in a single layer on a light-colored rimmed baking sheet. Bake at 350°F for 8 to 10 minutes, tossing or stirring occasionally. Depending on their oil content they could toast a little faster or a little more slowly than that, so check them often, and use your nose as well as the clock. Once you can smell the toasted nuts, they are usually ready to go.

Blanching

Blanching is a process used to remove the papery skins of nuts like almonds, hazelnuts, and pistachios. Almond skins are removed mostly for cosmetic reasons. Almond flour or frangipane made with blanched almonds is a creamy blond color rather than light brown. Hazelnut skins, though, are bitter and must be removed. You can either toast the nuts and rub off the skins or blanch them and pop them out of the skins.

To blanch nuts, put them in a pot, cover them with cold water, and bring the water to a boil, then immediately remove the pot from the heat and drain the nuts. You do not want to cook them at all.

Transfer the nuts to a clean dish towel. If the nuts are sturdy, like almonds and hazelnuts, you can wrap them up and rub them around in the towel to release the skins, then open the towel and pick out the skins. It's OK if you can't remove every bit of skin. Some nuts, such as pistachios, are too delicate to rub in a towel, so you must remove the skins by hand.

Grinding

To grind nuts or to make nut flour, use a food processor or a high-speed blender. I like to add a bit of sugar to the nuts in the food processor to ensure that they can be finely ground without turning into a paste. Be careful when using a high-speed blender, as the heat generated by the blade can cause the oils to separate out quickly. These blenders are great for making nut butter, but if you want ground nuts or nut flour, stop the machine frequently to check the texture. You can always grind the nuts finer if necessary, but you can't go backward.

Cocoa Basics

I've included cocoa in this chapter because I often use cocoa powder like flour, especially for gluten-free cakes, and, like flour, it adds bulk, flavor, and texture.

How do we get cocoa powder? First, cocoa beans are fermented, dried, and roasted. They are then shelled and ground into a liquid called cocoa liquor (also known as cocoa mass or cocoa solids). Cocoa powder is produced after all of the fat, called cocoa butter, is removed from the liquor and the solids are finely ground.

Sometimes some of the cocoa butter (or another less desirable but cheaper alternative) is added back, along with dairy and sugar, the product is further refined, and it becomes chocolate, another important ingredient in its own category altogether.

Dutch-Processed versus Natural Cocoa Powder

Dutch-processed cocoa powder has been treated with an alkali to neutralize its natural acidity; natural cocoa powder has not. Natural cocoa powder has a somewhat fruity flavor, while Dutch-processed is more mellow and chocolatey.

If there is no chemical leavener in the recipe (as in a custard, for example), feel free to use whichever cocoa powder you prefer. But if the recipe includes baking powder and/or baking soda, stick to the cocoa powder called for. Usually baking soda is used along with natural cocoa powder to neutralize its acidity.

Tempering Chocolate

Tempered chocolate has been processed so that the cocoa butter particles are aligned. It's shiny and snappy and stays solid at room temperature. If you're dipping a cookie in chocolate, such as the Chocolate and Coconut Meringue Cookies on page 103, it's not essential but it's nice if the chocolate is tempered.

I like two lazy methods for tempering. The first is called "seeding," and I do it in the microwave. You can do it too! Use bittersweet or semisweet chocolate disks or bars. (Milk and white chocolate can be tempered, but it's trickier with these, so I avoid it.) Do not use chips or candy melts, and stay away from chocolate with any signs of bloom. Bar chocolate and chocolate disks are always sold in temper, and you need them to do some of the work for you.

Conventional wisdom says to start with at least a pound of chopped chocolate, but I rarely do. Sometimes when I'm working with the disks, I don't even chop them. For the most consistent results, set about three quarters of your chopped chocolate in a microwave-safe bowl and melt it in shorts bursts, stirring after each one. Once the chocolate is completely melted, add the remaining chocolate a little bit at a time, stirring constantly, until it is all melted and the temperature has gone down to 88°F. The already aligned cocoa butter particles in the chopped chocolate will seed the rest of the chocolate. The second method I use is called the "incomplete melting" technique. I put all of the chocolate I need tempered in a microwave-safe bowl and melt it in short bursts, stirring occasionally. I stop heating it when about three quarters of it is melted. Then I stir, stir, stir, until the remaining chocolate melts and the temperature drops. Once you do this a few times, you too will be able to tell without a thermometer when the chocolate has fallen into temper. The mixture becomes a bit more fluid and slightly glossier. It's very satisfying! To test the chocolate, dip a room-temperature spoon into it and then set it down. The chocolate should harden and have a sheen in a few minutes.

Storing Chocolate

Store chocolate at room temperature (that is, below 70°F). Chocolate can absorb other flavors easily, so be sure to wrap it well for storage. Bloom is a white film that can appear on chocolate after it has been exposed to warmth or condensation. It may not have the perfect texture for eating out of hand, but it is fine to use for baking.

Percentages

Fine bar chocolate usually includes a percentage on the package. That number indicates the amount of cocoa mass, inclusive of cocoa butter, in relation to other additives, like lecithin, sugar, and milk. The higher the percentage, the darker the chocolate.

I avoid chocolate chips. They include stabilizers that help them keep their shape in baking, which makes melting them difficult. Higher-quality bar chocolate is easier to find than high-quality chips, and you can use it for everything. If you have to choose between keeping chip or bar chocolate on hand, go for bars. They are great for both snacking and baking.

	PERCENTAGE OF COCOA MASS	NOTES
Unsweetened Chocolate	100%	This is just cocoa liquor and cocoa butter. It's great for recipes where pure chocolate flavor is called for. Think brownies. A recipe made with unsweetened chocolate requires plenty of sugar and fat.
Bittersweet Chocolate	35% to 70% 35% is the minimum required for bittersweet chocolate. I like mine around 65%.	Bittersweet chocolate is intense but less bitter than unsweetened chocolate. It melts and tempers easily. This is my preferred chocolate for most baking, but the higher percentages can be a bit overpowering.
Semisweet Chocolate	The percentage can be much lower, but I like semisweet chocolate with 45% to 55% cocoa solids.	This is very similar to bittersweet but has more sugar. Semisweet is tasty in baked goods where the pieces of chocolate are larger and more obvious. A big pool of semisweet chocolate in a cookie, for example, is nicer than something darker.
Milk Chocolate	10% and up to 35%	Milk chocolate is made by adding milk solids, sugar, and fat to cocoa liquor. Look for high-quality milk chocolate for baking—some brands are bland and sugary. Milk chocolate is really best for custards, mousses, and similar desserts, as its flavor is muted in baked goods.
White Chocolate	0%	White chocolate is made with cocoa butter, milk, flavorings, and lecithin. Cocoa butter is expensive, so some companies use less delicious alternatives. Cheap white chocolate tastes terrible, so always seek out the real deal.

Any-Nut Frangipane

MAKES ABOUT 1¾ CUPS UNBAKED FRANGIPANE

Traditionally made with almonds, frangipane is a fragrant nut cream used to fill pastries and cookies. Try it in your next fruit galette, baked into the middle of a few stale croissants, swirled into a batch of Frangipane Brownies (page 168), or slathered over syrup-soaked brioche for Raspberry Pistachio Bostock (page 163). Once baked, frangipane becomes chewy and cake-like, thanks to the high ratio of eggs and sugar to nuts.

2 large (100 grams) eggs

1 cup (112 grams) nut flour, such as almond, hazelnut, pistachio, or walnut

½ cup (145 grams) packed light or dark brown sugar

4 tablespoons (½ stick; 57 grams) butter, softened

½ teaspoon kosher salt

Using store-bought nut flour means considerably less work for you and fewer dirty appliances.

In a medium bowl, whisk together the eggs. Add the nut flour, brown sugar, butter, and salt and beat with a wooden spoon or whisk, or with an electric mixer, until well combined. Use immediately.

To make frangipane using whole nuts, start by pulsing 1 cup (112 grams) of whole nuts with the sugar in a food processor until finely ground. Add the eggs, butter, and salt and process until smooth. You can use some nuts, like almonds or pistachios, with or without their skins; the flavor won't be noticeably different. But for a more refined look, use blanched nuts. And if you'd like to use hazelnuts, it's important to remove their bitter, papery skins. See page 146 for instructions.

Nut Paste

MAKES ABOUT 12 OUNCES

I love to swirl nut paste into butter cake batters or bake it into Raspberry and Almond Bear Claws (page 203) or Roulés aux Raisins with Pistachio Cream (page 194). Once you start with nut paste, it's hard to stop. You'll be spreading this ambrosia on your morning toast before you know it.

1¼ cups (175 grams) nuts

1½ cups (180 grams) confectioners' sugar

  1 large (30 grams) egg white

    Pinch of kosher salt

1½ teaspoons pure vanilla extract

¼ teaspoon pure almond extract

While blanching the nuts isn't essential, it does make for a cleaner flavor and prettier color, especially when it comes to pistachios. See page 146 for instructions.

In the bowl of a food processor, combine the nuts, confectioners' sugar, egg white, and salt and process until smooth, about 4 minutes. Add the vanilla and almond extracts and process to combine. The paste can be stored, well wrapped in plastic wrap, in the fridge for up to 1 month or in the freezer for up to 3 months.

Different nuts, with their varying fat contents, will result in pastes with different consistencies. If you want the paste to be thinner, simply add a teaspoon or two of warm water to the mixture as you run the food processor.

Banana Crumb Cake

SERVES 8 TO 10

I believe that for crumb cake the proper ratio of crumb to cake is 50:50. Finely milled low-protein cake flour ensures that this cake has a light and tender crumb. Sour cream, which inhibits gluten formation, also helps.

CRUMB

- 10 tablespoons (1¼ sticks; 141 grams) butter, melted and still warm, plus butter for the pan
- 1¾ cups (233 grams) cake flour
- ⅓ cup (67 grams) packed light or dark brown sugar
- ¼ cup (50 grams) granulated sugar
- 1 teaspoon ground cinnamon
- ½ teaspoon kosher salt

CAKE

- 1½ cups (200 grams) cake flour
- ½ teaspoon baking soda
- ½ teaspoon kosher salt
- ¾ cup (216 grams) mashed banana (from about 2 bananas)
- ⅓ cup (80 grams) sour cream, at room temperature
- 2 teaspoons vanilla extract
- 6 tablespoons (¾ stick; 85 grams) butter, at room temperature
- ⅓ cup (67 grams) packed light or dark brown sugar
- 1 large (50 grams) egg, at room temperature
- 1 large (20 grams) egg yolk, at room temperature
- ⅔ cup (94 grams) semisweet chocolate, coarsely chopped

Confectioners' sugar for dusting

Melted butter makes the crunchiest crumb topping.

To save overripe bananas, peel them and freeze in an airtight container. If you want to be very organized, you can freeze mashed bananas in 1-cup portions.

Preheat the oven to 350°F. Butter an 8-inch square baking pan and line with parchment paper, leaving a 2-inch overhang on two opposite sides.

PREPARE THE CRUMB. In a medium bowl, whisk together the flour, brown sugar, granulated sugar, cinnamon, and salt. Add the melted butter and stir to combine. Set aside.

PREPARE THE CAKE. In a large bowl, whisk together the flour, baking soda, and salt. In a small bowl, whisk together the banana, sour cream, and vanilla.

In a medium bowl, with an electric mixer on medium speed, beat together the butter and brown sugar until fluffy, about 3 minutes. Add the egg and egg yolk and beat to combine.

Beat in half of the flour mixture. Beat in the banana mixture and then finish with the remaining dry ingredients. Fold in the chocolate, if using.

Add the batter to the prepared pan and spread evenly. Top with the crumb mixture, squeezing it into various-sized clumps as you add it.

Bake the cake until a toothpick inserted into the center comes out with a few moist crumbs attached, 30 to 35 minutes. Let cool completely in the pan on a rack.

To serve, cut the cake into squares and dust with confectioners' sugar.

Store leftovers in an airtight container at room temperature for up to 5 days, or in the freezer for 1 month. Thaw at room temperature to serve.

Chocolate-Cherry Marzipan Biscotti

MAKES ABOUT 45 BISCOTTI

Tart dried cherries, rather than sweet dried cherries, are essential for balancing the sweetness of the marzipan in these crisp cookies. If you don't want to use store-bought marzipan, you can make these with homemade almond paste (page 151). When baked, the little pieces of marzipan in the biscotti are transformed into golden brown, chewy, almond-flavored nuggets.

7 ounces (198 grams) marzipan or Nut Paste (page 151) made with almonds

1 teaspoon confectioners' sugar

2 cups (272 grams) all-purpose flour

¾ cup (63 grams) Dutch-processed cocoa powder

2 teaspoons baking powder

1 teaspoon kosher salt

1¼ cups (250 grams) granulated sugar

8 tablespoons (1 stick; 113 grams) butter, at room temperature

3 large (150 grams) eggs

1 cup (142 grams) tart dried cherries

⅔ cup (94 grams) semisweet chocolate, coarsely chopped

1 large (30 grams) egg white, beaten

Sanding sugar for sprinkling (optional)

Dutch-processed cocoa makes deep, dark-chocolatey biscotti.

Use an oiled knife to cut the marzipan or almond paste into ¼-inch cubes. Toss the marzipan or almond paste with the confectioners' sugar to separate the cubes. Freeze for at least 20 minutes.

Preheat the oven to 350°F, with the racks in the upper and lower thirds of the oven. Line two rimmed baking sheets with parchment paper.

In a medium bowl, whisk together the flour, cocoa powder, baking powder, and salt.

In a large bowl, with an electric mixer on medium, beat the sugar and butter until fluffy. Add the eggs one at a time, beating until combined after each addition. Add the flour mixture and beat until just combined. Add the cherries, chocolate, and marzipan or almond paste and stir to combine, trying not to mash the cubes of nut paste.

Tip the dough out and divide it in half. Roll each half into a 12-inch-long log and transfer the logs to one of the prepared baking sheet, spacing them at least 2 inches apart. Using your fingers, gently press down on the top of each log so

that it is about 2 inches wide. Brush the tops of the logs with the egg white. Sprinkle the tops with sanding sugar, if using.

Bake the logs until puffed and set, 25 to 28 minutes. The tops will look dry and crackly. Transfer the baking sheet to a rack to cool completely. Reduce the oven temperature to 325°F.

Transfer the logs to a cutting board. With an oiled sharp chef's knife, cut each log into scant ½-inch slices on a slight bias. (Do not use a serrated knife.) The cookies will be very delicate at this point. Carefully transfer the slices to the parchment-lined baking sheets.

Bake the biscotti until they are crisp, 20 to 24 minutes, rotating the sheets halfway through. Transfer the sheets to racks to cool completely.

Biscotti freeze beautifully. Save extras in an airtight container in the freezer for up to 3 months. You can thaw them at room temperature before serving, but I think they taste terrific frozen.

Dip your fingers in water before shaping the sticky dough logs.

Gianduja Rugelach

Gianduja, an Italian confection made of hazelnuts and chocolate, is used to fill these simple but delicious rugelach.

DOUGH

- 8 tablespoons (1 stick; 113 grams) cold butter, cut into pieces
- 4 ounces (113 grams) cream cheese, cool but not cold
- 2 tablespoons (25 grams) granulated sugar
- 1½ teaspoons pure vanilla extract
- ½ teaspoon kosher salt
- ¾ cup (102 grams) all-purpose flour

GIANDUJA FILLING

- ¼ cup (50 grams) packed light brown sugar
- ½ cup (66 grams) hazelnuts, toasted and skinned
- ¾ cup (105 grams) bittersweet chocolate, chopped
- 2 tablespoons (¼ stick; 28 grams) butter
- ½ teaspoon kosher salt

TO FINISH

- 1 large (50 grams) egg, beaten
- Sanding sugar for sprinkling

PREPARE THE DOUGH. In a large bowl, with an electric mixer on medium speed, beat the butter, cream cheese, sugar, vanilla, and salt until fluffy, about 2 minutes. Add the flour and beat until just evenly moistened. Don't overmix.

Tip the dough out onto a piece of plastic wrap and bring it together in a cohesive mass. Divide the dough into 4 portions. Wrap each one in plastic wrap and shape into a square. Refrigerate the dough for at least 2 hours, and up to 3 days.

PREPARE THE GIANDUJA FILLING. Combine the brown sugar and hazelnuts in a blender or food processor and process until the nuts are very finely chopped.

In a medium microwave-safe bowl, melt the chocolate and butter in the microwave in short bursts, stirring after each burst. Add the nut mixture to the chocolate mixture and stir in the salt.

Place one square of dough between two pieces of parchment paper and roll it out into a 12 x 6-inch rectangle. Remove the top piece of parchment and spread a quarter of the filling over the dough, leaving a ¼-inch border. Starting with a long edge, roll the dough

up into a tight cylinder. You can use the parchment paper to help the dough along. If it gets too soft, pop it into the fridge to chill for a few minutes. Wrap the cylinder in the parchment and chill for at least 30 minutes. Repeat with the remaining dough squares and filling.

Preheat the oven to 375°F, with the racks in the upper and lower thirds of the oven. Line two rimmed baking sheets with parchment paper.

Brush each log with the beaten egg and sprinkle with sanding sugar. Cut each log into 1½-inch pieces and place them on the prepared sheets, leaving an inch between them.

Bake until the rugelach are puffed and golden brown, 20 to 25 minutes, rotating the sheets halfway through. Some of the filling will spill out; it always happens. Transfer the sheets to a rack to cool.

The rugelach can be stored in an airtight container at room temperature for up to 1 week or in the freezer for up to 1 month.

The filling that tends to seep out of the rugelach bakes up crisp and tasty. If it clings to the rugelach, just leave it; it will taste of caramel and chocolate. Or do as I do, and save it to crumble over a bowl of ice cream or yogurt.

FLOURS, NUTS & COCOA 157

Maple Tahini Chocolate Skillet Cake

SERVES 16

This casual cake can make a regular Wednesday night special.

- ½ cup (112 grams) tahini
- 2 tablespoons (39 grams) maple syrup
- 8 tablespoons (1 stick; 113 grams) butter, melted and slightly cooled
- 1 cup (200 grams) packed dark brown sugar
- 2 large (100 grams) eggs
- 2 teaspoons pure vanilla extract
- ¾ cup (102 grams) all-purpose flour
- ¾ cup (63 grams) Dutch-processed cocoa powder
- ½ teaspoon baking powder
- ¾ teaspoon kosher salt
- Coffee ice cream for serving (optional)

Preheat the oven to 350°F.

In a small bowl, mix together the tahini and maple syrup.

In an 8-inch ovenproof skillet, melt the butter. Remove from the heat and let cool a bit.

Whisk the brown sugar into the butter, then whisk in the eggs one at a time. Whisk in the vanilla. Add the flour, cocoa, baking powder, and salt and whisk vigorously to combine. Smooth the top of the batter.

Dollop the tahini mixture all over the top of the batter and then use a toothpick or a butter knife to swirl it in a decorative pattern. Bake until the cake is just set and a toothpick inserted into the center comes out with a few moist crumbs attached, about 20 minutes. (It's better to underbake than overbake this cake.) Set the pan on a rack to cool slightly.

Serve the cake warm, topped with ice cream, if wanted. Store leftovers in an airtight container at room temperature for up 3 days.

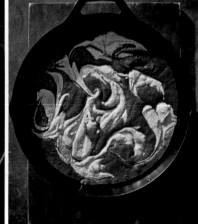

Chocolate Ginger Scones

MAKES 9 SCONES

Black pepper and ginger give these deeply chocolatey scones a sophisticated bite.

- 1 large (50 grams) egg
- ¾ cup (180 grams) heavy cream, plus 3 tablespoons (44 grams)
- 2 cups (272 grams) all-purpose flour, plus more for the parchment paper
- ⅓ cup (25 grams) Dutch-processed cocoa powder
- 1 tablespoon (12 grams) baking powder
- ½ teaspoon freshly ground black pepper
- ¼ teaspoon baking soda
- ½ teaspoon kosher salt
- ½ cup (100 grams) granulated sugar
- 8 tablespoons (1 stick; 113 grams) butter, frozen
- ¾ cup (105 grams) semisweet chocolate, chopped
- ½ cup (84 grams) chopped crystallized ginger
- Sanding sugar for sprinkling
- Mascarpone cheese for serving (optional)

You want the butter to be very cold so that instead of seeping out of the dough, it creates steam in the oven.

In a small bowl, whisk together the egg and the ¾ cup cream.

In a large bowl, whisk together the flour, cocoa powder, baking powder, pepper, baking soda, salt, and granulated sugar. Using a box grater, grate the butter into the flour. Add the chocolate and ginger and toss to combine. Add the cream mixture to the flour mixture and mix with a fork just until a shaggy dough forms. Add 1 to 2 tablespoons more cream if necessary.

Tip the dough out onto a lightly floured piece of parchment paper and pat into a 6-inch square.

With a sharp knife, cut the dough into 9 squares. Arrange the squares on a baking sheet or a plate. Freeze for 20 minutes. (You can freeze the unbaked scones in an airtight container for up to 1 month. Bake from frozen, but increase the baking time by a few minutes.)

Preheat the oven to 400°F. Line a rimmed baking sheet with parchment paper.

Brush the tops of the frozen squares of dough with the 3 tablespoons cream and sprinkle with sanding sugar. Transfer to the prepared baking sheet and bake until a toothpick inserted into the center of a scone comes out with a few moist crumbs attached, 20 to 22 minutes. Let the scones cool completely on the sheet on a rack.

Split the scones and slather them with mascarpone, if wanted, to serve. The scones are best the day they're made.

There may be a bit of the dry mixture visible after you add the liquid. That's OK! It's better to undermix slightly and keep the butter cold than to overmix.

Cutting the dough for scones or biscuits into squares avoids wasting dough.

Raspberry Pistachio Bostock

SERVES 6

Bostock, syrup-soaked toast topped with frangipane and baked, is like the most indulgent (and wonderful) French toast you've ever dreamed of. And it practically demands improvisation. Use any nut you'd like for the frangipane. Change the chocolate or swap the raspberries out for other fruits. You could even change the flavors in the syrup. Cardamom or vanilla beans would be nice. You need a base of enriched bread, and then the sky's the limit.

SYRUP

- ½ cup (100 grams) granulated sugar
- ½ cup (120 grams) water
- 6 strips orange zest
- 2 tablespoons (16 grams) fresh orange juice

PISTACHIO FRANGIPANE

- ½ cup (100 grams) granulated sugar
- ½ cup (75 grams) raw pistachios
- 8 tablespoons (1 stick; 113 grams) butter, cut into pieces, at room temperature
- 1 large (50 grams) egg, at room temperature
- 1 tablespoon (9 grams) all-purpose flour
- ¼ teaspoon almond extract
- Pinch of kosher salt

TO ASSEMBLE

- Six 1½-inch slices brioche or challah
- 1 cup (120 grams) fresh raspberries
- 2 tablespoons (18 grams) chopped milk chocolate

TO FINISH

- Confectioners' sugar for dusting
- Chopped pistachios for sprinkling

I highly recommend removing the pistachio skins; the pistachio flavor will be much cleaner. See page 146 for instructions on blanching pistachios.

Preheat the oven to 350°F. Line a rimmed baking sheet with parchment paper.

PREPARE THE SYRUP. In a small saucepan, combine the sugar, water, and orange zest, bring to a simmer, and cook until the mixture is reduced and syrupy and well flavored with the zest, about 5 minutes, stirring occasionally. Remove from the heat and add the orange juice.

PREPARE THE PISTACHIO FRANGIPANE. In the bowl of a food processor or high-speed blender, combine the sugar and pistachios and pulse until the nuts are very finely ground. Add the butter, egg, flour, almond extract, and salt and pulse until a smooth paste forms.

ASSEMBLE THE BOSTOCK. Set the slices of brioche on the prepared baking sheet. Using a pastry brush, evenly coat the slices with the orange syrup. Divide the frangipane among the slices of bread and spread it evenly over the tops. Divide the raspberries evenly among the slices and scatter the chocolate over the top.

Bake until the frangipane is golden brown and completely set, 30 to 35 minutes. Remove from the oven and let cool slightly.

Serve the bostock warm, dusted with confectioners' sugar and sprinkled with pistachios. Bostock is best the day it's made.

Lighter silicone pastry brushes work well for delicate yeasted pastries where the coarseness of natural bristles could deflate the dough. But for something like this, where you want to really soak the bread, a traditional brush with natural bristles is the way to go. These do sometimes leave bristles behind, especially when they get older, so give the slices of bread a once-over before topping with the frangipane.

Toasted Coconut and Pecan Financiers

MAKES 12 FINANCIERS

Financiers are usually made with almonds or hazelnuts, but these pecan and coconut financiers are part macaroon. They are usually baked in special molds, but Dorie Greenspan taught me this muffin pan method, and I've never looked back.

- 4 tablespoons (½ stick; 57 grams) butter, melted and slightly cooled, plus more for the pan
- ½ cup (47 grams) unsweetened shredded coconut
- ½ cup (55 grams) pecan halves
- ⅓ cup (67 grams) granulated sugar
- 2 tablespoons (17 grams) all-purpose flour
- Pinch of kosher salt
- 2 large (60 grams) egg whites
- ½ teaspoon pure vanilla extract
- 2 tablespoons (40 grams) raspberry jam

There is less butter in this financier recipe than in most because pecans and coconut are so full of delicious fat. Do not swap in other nuts.

Preheat the oven to 350°F. Butter a 12-cup mini-muffin pan. Line a rimmed baking sheet with parchment paper.

Spread the coconut and pecans, next to each other, on the prepared baking sheet and toast in the oven until both are lightly browned, 6 to 8 minutes, stirring halfway through and keeping a close watch toward the end. Both coconut and pecans can go from perfectly toasted to burnt in less than a minute. Remove from the oven and let cool.

Combine the cooled pecans and the sugar in the bowl of a food processor or blender and pulse until the pecans are finely ground. Transfer to a medium bowl.

Use your fingertips to rub the coconut with the pecan mixture to break it down into small pieces. Add the flour and salt and whisk to combine. Whisk in the egg whites and vanilla, then whisk in the melted butter.

Divide the batter evenly among the prepared muffin cups. (A small cookie scoop makes easy work of filling the muffin cups evenly.) Tap the pan on the countertop to smooth the tops. Set a small dollop (½ teaspoon) of jam in the center of each financier.

Bake until the cakes spring back when pressed gently in the center, 18 to 20 minutes. Pop them out of the pan, using a small offset spatula or knife to loosen the edges if needed, and transfer to a rack to cool completely.

The financiers can be stored in an airtight container at room temperature for up to 5 days, or in the freezer for 1 month.

Use a light-colored baking sheet to toast the coconut and nuts. They will be less likely to burn and you can keep a better eye on the color as it changes.

A drizzle of melted chocolate over each financier wouldn't hurt.

Almond-Apricot Wafer Sandwiches

MAKES ABOUT 18 SANDWICH COOKIES

These wafers are like lacy Florentine cookies, but with a bit less sugar and a lot more chew. They remind me of granola with some chocolate thrown in for fun.

2 cups (284 grams) roasted salted almonds, finely chopped in a food processor

½ cup (80 grams) dried apricots, finely chopped

½ cup (68 grams) all-purpose flour

½ cup (100 grams) granulated sugar, plus more for the glass

6 tablespoons (¾ stick; 85 grams) butter

⅓ cup (77 grams) heavy cream

2 tablespoons (42 grams) Lyle's Golden Syrup or honey

½ teaspoon kosher salt

1¼ cups (175 grams) bittersweet chocolate, melted

In a medium bowl, combine the almonds, apricots, and flour, tossing to mix.

In a small saucepan, combine the sugar, butter, heavy cream, golden syrup or honey, and salt, bring to a boil over medium-high heat, and cook for 1 minute. Immediately pour the sugar mixture over the almond mixture and stir to combine. Let stand until slightly cooled, about 10 minutes.

Preheat the oven to 350°F. Line two rimmed baking sheets with parchment paper.

Scoop the batter by scant 1-tablespoon mounds and set 5 on each prepared baking sheet. Using the flat bottom of a sugar-dusted glass, smoosh the cookies to flatten them.

Bake until the cookies are golden brown and set, 6 to 8 minutes. Transfer the cookies, on the parchment, to a rack to cool completely. Repeat with the remaining batter, rotating in the unused baking sheet and replacing parchment as needed.

Spread a bit of the melted chocolate on the flat side of one cookie. Top with another cookie, flat side down. Repeat with the remaining cookies and chocolate. Let set at room temperature before serving.

The cookies can be stored in an airtight container at room temperature for up to 5 days.

For easy filling, transfer the chocolate to a resealable plastic bag, snip off one of the bottom corners, and pipe a dollop of chocolate onto half of the cookies.

Don't skip the smooshing step: besides being fun, it's the only way that these cookies will flatten.

Frangipane Brownies

MAKES 9 BROWNIES

The chewy, nutty frangipane swirl gives these brownies an edge of sophistication.

- 8 tablespoons (1 stick; 113 grams) butter, plus more for the pan
- 1 cup (200 grams) granulated sugar
- 2 large (100 grams) eggs
- 1½ teaspoons pure vanilla extract
- ½ cup (68 grams) all-purpose flour
- ¾ cup (63 grams) Dutch-processed or natural cocoa powder
- ¼ teaspoon baking powder
- Pinch of kosher salt

- 1 recipe Any-Nut Frangipane (page 150)

Using cocoa powder rather than melted chocolate makes brownies that live somewhere between cakey and chewy. Melted chocolate, with its added fat and sugar, makes dense, fudgy brownies.

Preheat the oven to 350°F. Butter an 8-inch square baking pan and line it with parchment paper, leaving a 2-inch overhang on two opposite sides.

In a medium saucepan, combine the butter and sugar and heat over medium until the butter is melted. Remove from the heat and whisk vigorously until well combined. Let the mixture cool a bit.

One at a time, whisk the eggs into the butter mixture. Whisk in the vanilla. Add the flour, cocoa powder, baking powder, and salt and stir to combine. Set aside.

Alternate scoops of the brownie batter and the frangipane in the prepared pan, then swirl the two together with a butter knife.

Bake until the top of the brownie looks dry and set and a toothpick inserted into the center comes out with a few moist crumbs attached, 28 to 32 minutes. Remove from the oven and transfer to a rack to cool.

Cut the brownies into squares to serve. They can be stored in an airtight container at room temperature for up to 3 days, or in the freezer for up to 1 month. Thaw at room temperature before serving.

I think a butter knife makes the best tool for swirling. A skewer is too thin to make good swirls and a spatula is too wide.

Berry-Cottage Cheese Skillet Cake

SERVES 8

This adaptable weeknight cake takes to other fruits very well. Use whatever fruit you're in the mood for, matching the prepped weight with that of the berries.

- 8 tablespoons (1 stick; 113 grams) butter, at room temperature, plus more for the skillet
- 1½ cups (204 grams) all-purpose flour
- 1 teaspoon baking powder
- ¾ teaspoon ground cinnamon
- ½ teaspoon kosher salt
- ¾ cup (150 grams) packed light or dark brown sugar
- ½ cup (132 grams) full-fat cottage cheese, at room temperature
- 2 large (100 grams) eggs
- 1 large (80 grams) egg yolk
- ¼ cup (61 grams) whole milk, at room temperature
- 1½ teaspoons pure vanilla extract
- 1½ cups (200 grams) mixed fresh berries
- ½ cup (50 grams) sliced almonds, lightly toasted
- Demerara or sanding sugar for sprinkling

Cottage cheese does the same work as buttermilk and yogurt, adding tang, moisture, and richness to cakes. Always use high-quality full-fat cottage cheese—the kind you'd be happy to eat with a spoon.

Don't wash delicate berries until just before you use them. The added moisture can encourage rot. Swish them around in a bowl of water and then transfer them to a paper towel–lined rimmed baking sheet. Gently shake the pan from side to side to roll the berries around on the paper and get rid of excess moisture.

Sliced almonds with their skins, if you can find them, make for a pretty topping.

Preheat the oven to 350°F. Butter a 10-inch ovenproof skillet.

In a medium bowl, whisk together the flour, baking powder, cinnamon, and salt.

In a large bowl, with an electric mixer on medium speed, beat together the brown sugar, butter, and cottage cheese until almost smooth. (Some cottage cheese curds may still be visible. That's OK!) Add the eggs one at a time and then the egg yolk, beating well after each addition. Beat in the milk and vanilla. Add the flour mixture and beat just until combined. Do not overmix. Fold in about half of the berries.

Transfer the batter to the prepared pan and smooth the top. Top with the remaining berries. Top with the almonds and a generous sprinkle of demerara or sanding sugar.

Bake until a toothpick inserted into the center of the cake comes out with a few moist crumbs attached, 25 to 28 minutes. Serve warm, scooping the cake out of the pan, or at room temperature, cut into slices.

Store leftovers, covered, at room temperature for up to 3 days.

Pistachio-Stuffed Chocolate Crinkle Cookies

MAKES 18 COOKIES

These familiar-looking chocolate crinkle cookies actually have a hidden secret.

- 1 cup (136 grams) all-purpose flour
- ⅔ cup (57 grams) Dutch-processed cocoa powder
- 1 teaspoon baking soda
- ½ teaspoon kosher salt
- 8 tablespoons (1 stick; 113 grams) butter, softened
- ½ cup (100 grams) granulated sugar
- ½ cup (100 grams) packed light or dark brown sugar
- 1 large (50 grams) egg, at room temperature
- 2 teaspoons pure vanilla extract
- ½ recipe Nut Paste (page 151) made with pistachios

TO FINISH

- Granulated sugar
- Confectioners' sugar

Almond or hazelnut paste would be nice too.

Preheat the oven to 350°F, with the racks in the upper and lower thirds of the oven. Line two rimmed baking sheets with parchment paper.

In a medium bowl, whisk together the flour, cocoa, baking soda, and salt.

In a large bowl, with an electric mixer on medium speed, beat the butter, granulated sugar, and brown sugar until fluffy, about 4 minutes. Add the egg and vanilla and beat to combine. Add the flour mixture and beat just until combined.

Cut the pistachio paste into 18 equal pieces. Portion the dough into 1-tablespoon scoops on a work surface. Set a piece of pistachio paste onto half of the scoops of dough. Top each with another dough scoop and roll the dough into a ball enclosing the paste completely. Set the granulated sugar and confectioners' sugar in two shallow bowls. Roll each ball in the granulated sugar and then in the confectioners' sugar and set the balls on the prepared sheets at least 1 inch apart, about 9 cookies per sheet.

Bake the cookies until the tops look cracked and dry, 12 to 15 minutes, rotating the sheets halfway through. Transfer to a rack to cool completely.

The cookies can be stored in an airtight container at room temperature for up to 3 days, or in the freezer for 1 month.

For perfectly round cookies, place a larger round cookie cutter around one warm cookie. Spin the cutter carefully so that the cookie hits the sides of the cutter and rounds itself out. Repeat with the remaining cookies.

Cook's Illustrated taught me that in order to have great crinkles and clean white confectioners' sugar, you should roll crinkle cookies in granulated sugar first. The granulated sugar effectively dries out the outsides of the cookies, which both creates a barrier to keep the confectioners' sugar white and results in nice cracks as the cookies bake.

Yeast

Yeast is an essential ingredient in any baker's pantry. It's responsible for the fermentation of dough, which contributes to both the structure and the flavor of the final bake. I favor enriched doughs, those that include butter, sugar, milk, and eggs, which are used for things like cinnamon buns and babka. They're a bit more forgiving than lean doughs, which are used for sourdough breads and baguettes. But trust me, I haven't always been entirely successful with these either. As a kid, my first tries with yeast doughs were utter failures—it seemed that nothing I ever mixed rose properly. I remember spending one early sweet-bun experiment sitting on the central heating vent in our living room cradling a bowl of cold dough with an unzipped sleeping bag over my head. Simply setting it in a warm spot wasn't working so I was trying to create an even warmer (and cozier)

spot. Every time the hot air whooshed up, the bag would inflate over my head and I would lie down with the bowl of dough on my lap, desperately trying to warm it up and get it to puff. I ended up with nothing more than a flat dough and a hot backside.

The truth is that baker's yeast, the kind you buy at the supermarket, is easy to manipulate. It was developed to be exactly that. Wild yeasts, those that are harnessed for sourdough, can be trickier to manage and often lead to inconsistent results. But if you know how to handle it, regular yeast is very reliable. No sleeping bags required.

I suspect my problem then was not with the ambient temperature of my house, but with the age of the yeast. It's true that commercial yeast is dependable, but there are a few important things to know.

Yeast Basics

Yeast is a single-celled organism that, under the right conditions, will consume the sugars in a dough and produce alcohol and carbon dioxide. When that carbon dioxide is trapped within the glutinous network of bread dough, it expands, and the dough rises. It simply needs food and a warm, moist environment for eating it.

At the Supermarket

FRESH YEAST: Fresh yeast is sold in little blocks in the refrigerated section of the supermarket. It should be moist and creamy, not dry or crumbly, with a pleasant yeasty smell. Fresh yeast must be proofed in warm liquid with a bit of sugar before use. It's not my go-to yeast, because it goes bad quickly.
ACTIVE DRY YEAST: This is fresh yeast that's been compressed and dried, giving it a longer shelf life. You'll find it most often in little ¼-ounce (2¼-teaspoon) packets. If unopened, the packets don't need to be refrigerated, but they will start to lose potency once opened, so pop them in the fridge after that. I developed the recipes in this book using active dry yeast.

Many bakers say that active dry yeast needs to be proofed before adding it to a dough. I don't find that to be true. In most of these recipes, I've included a proofing step simply to give you an opportunity to check the yeast and make sure it is still potent. If you're confident that your yeast is still fresh, go ahead and add it directly to your flour mixture, along with any liquid called for in the proofing step. Red Star Yeast is my favorite brand because, unlike others, it will dissolve completely in the dough even without proofing it in liquid first.

INSTANT YEAST: Instant yeast has been compressed, dried, and milled finer than active dry yeast. It was designed to be added directly to a flour or other mixture without proofing. I don't use instant yeast, and I don't recommend it. My doughs seem to proof a little too quickly with it, and they don't develop a good flavor or texture. I also find that with instant yeast, I can't slow the rise on a dough with refrigeration, which is sometimes necessary to break the process down over a few days or to develop flavor, and achieve consistent results. In general, instant yeast doesn't do anything that active dry yeast can't do, and it produces inferior results. You can swap in an equal amount of active dry yeast for instant yeast in most recipes that call for instant, but you'll need to increase the rise time.

The Proof

Yeasted Dough Best Practices

- Check the sell-by date, and discard any yeast you have that is past its prime.

- Use an instant-read thermometer to check the liquid when you first start making yeast breads until you've gotten a good feel for the correct temperature for proofing yeast. Aim for between 110°F and 115°F.

- Don't agitate the yeast much once you've added it to the warm liquid and sugar (or honey) mixture. Vigorous whisking seems to make yeast unhappy, or least sluggish.

- Many recipes advise bakers to keep the dough away from any drafts while it rises, but air currents aren't exactly the issue—it's temperature. For dependable results, keep your dough somewhere consistently warm. A good average temperature for rising dough is around 80°F. If the dough is laminated with butter, a little cooler is better. Aim for about 70°F.

- Make sure to keep the dough covered so that the surface doesn't dry out, form a crust, and thereby inhibit the rise.

- When you're starting out, I suggest mixing a sweet yeast dough by hand so that you can get a real feel for it.

- Before setting a dough aside for its first rise, it's a good idea to fold it over itself at 12, 3, 6, and 9 o'clock and then turn it over and shape it into a neat ball. Folding it over like this helps the yeast thrive. It will also be easier to tell if the dough has risen properly if it's been shaped nicely.

Create a proofing box

Some ovens come with a "proof" setting. This wonderful option keeps the oven temperature at around 80°F so you can proof your dough in a controlled setting. You can create a similar environment by putting a baking pan full of boiling-hot water on the lower oven rack, placing the dough, in a lightly covered bowl on the top rack, and keeping the oven door closed.

How do you know when a dough is ready to bake?

Determining when a risen dough is ready is the trickiest part of baking with yeast. The more often you do it, though, the easier it will be to tell.

First and foremost, check the dough, not the clock. Most recipes give a rising time as a guideline, but it's much more important to see what the dough is doing. Keep in mind that a dough made with extra butter and sugar will take longer to rise, especially if it's had a rest in the refrigerator—it may take hours. Second, it's very hard to judge whether a dough has actually grown to double its original size. Shaped doughs can be particularly hard to judge. Snap a picture of the dough with your cell phone and set a time to come back and compare. I also like to write the time on the plastic wrap covering the dough with a Sharpie.

To check if the dough is ready, first give the bowl a gentle shake. Properly proofed dough will jiggle a bit; underproofed dough will not. Second, press an indentation into the dough with your finger. If it springs back slowly, it's ready; if it bounces back fast, the dough needs more time. If it doesn't bounce back at all, the dough might be overproofed. A properly proofed dough will be somewhat rounded, not flat.

If you're on the first rise of the dough, before it's been shaped, and you feel that it's gone too far, you can usually save it. Expel the gas by folding the dough over itself a few times and then set it aside to rise again. If it's a shaped dough on its second rise, you don't have many options. Bake it anyway and try again another day. It won't be perfect, but I bet it will still be pretty tasty.

Slow Down

Yeasted dough may take a bit of time to prepare, but thankfully it's easy to adapt it to your own schedule. To break a recipe up over a couple days, so that you aren't babysitting a dough for your whole free Saturday, simply let the dough complete its first rise in the fridge, rather than at room temperature. In the fridge, this rise will take longer. You can leave the dough in the fridge, covered tightly, for up to 48 hours. Shape the dough while it's still cold and then let it complete its final rise at room temperature. Because the dough will be cold, this rise will take a while. Remember to watch the dough, not the clock.

Basic Enriched Sweet Dough

MAKES ENOUGH FOR 12 BUNS

This is my favorite dough. It's versatile and easy to make, and it feels like a downy puppy belly after it's risen. Use it to make the Apricot Cardamom Buns (page 184), Chocolate Sesame Swirl Bread (page 186), the Ginger Brûlée Doughnuts (page 190), and whatever else you can dream up!

I like to add a couple of extra egg yolks to my enriched doughs. I find that they help achieve a soft and fluffy bread. They also give the dough an appealing buttery yellow color. And egg yolks contain lecithin, an emulsifier that author Shirley Corriher says enhances the "keeping quality" of bread. Win, win, win.

- ½ cup (120 grams) whole milk, warmed to 110°F to 120°F
- 1½ teaspoons active dry yeast
- ¼ cup (50 grams) plus 1 teaspoon granulated sugar
- 2¼ cups (306 grams) all-purpose flour, plus more as needed
- 1 large (50 grams) egg
- 2 large (40 grams) egg yolks
- ½ teaspoon kosher salt
- 4 tablespoons (½ stick; 57 grams) butter, cut into ½-inch cubes, at room temperature

Pour the milk into a small bowl. Stir in the yeast and 1 teaspoon of the sugar and let stand until foamy, about 5 minutes.

In the bowl of a stand mixer fitted with the paddle attachment, blend the remaining ¼ cup sugar, the flour, the egg and egg yolks, and salt on low speed.

Switch to the dough hook and knead the mixture on low speed until a cohesive dough forms and becomes stretchy, about 4 minutes. Add the butter a piece or two at a time. It may look as if it's not getting in there, but don't worry, it will; just keep adding the butter and kneading it in. Once all the butter is incorporated, increase the speed to medium and knead the dough for another few minutes, or until it is smooth and elastic. If you decide to make the dough by hand, you may want to use a dough scraper in one hand to help incorporate the butter. The dough will be sticky. Don't add extra flour.

Scrape down the sides of the bowl and form the dough into a ball. Cover and let stand at room temperature until doubled in size, about 2 hours.

Tip the dough out onto a work surface and gently fold it over itself at 12, 3, 6, and 9 o'clock, then flip it over and form it into a tight ball. Return the dough to the bowl, cover tightly, and transfer to the fridge for the second rise. Let the dough rest and rise in the fridge for at least 4 hours, and up to 2 days, before using.

The butter will coat the flour proteins and slow down the development of gluten, which is the reason I have you knead the dough for a couple of minutes before adding the butter. That said, kneading doesn't have to be an all-day affair. Even if the dough isn't perfectly smooth at the end, it will sort itself out as it rests and rises.

Folding and shaping the dough into a tight ball before each rest and rise allows it to trap gases more effectively. It also makes the final shaping easier by aligning the gluten strands.

A slow second rise in the fridge allows for more flavor development, and chilling the dough makes it easier to work with.

Rough Laminated Yeasted Dough

Instead of wrapping dough around a butter block and rolling and folding it, as in making classic puff pastry, this rough version calls for tossing cold sliced butter into the flour and then rolling and folding it. The process is considerably easier and still produces lovely pastries. And here's an important secret: even if the final product is not exactly the flaky masterpiece you were hoping for, it will still taste great.

- 1½ cups (204 grams) all-purpose flour, plus more for the work surface and rolling pin
- 2 tablespoons (25 grams) granulated sugar
- 2 teaspoons active dry yeast
- ¾ teaspoon kosher salt
- 16 tablespoons (2 sticks; 226 grams) cold butter, cut into thin slices
- 1 large (50 grams) egg
- ¼ cup (60 grams) cold whole milk
- 2 tablespoons (30 grams) water

The milk adds richness and encourages browning.

In a large bowl, combine the flour, sugar, yeast, and salt. Add the butter and toss to combine.

In a small bowl, whisk together the egg, milk, and water. Add to the flour mixture and, using a butter knife, fold the mixture until the flour is evenly moistened. Take care to keep the butter pieces whole.

Tip the dough out onto a piece of plastic wrap, shape into a small rectangle, and wrap well in plastic wrap. Chill for at least 2 hours, and up to 2 days.

Let the dough sit at room temperature for a few minutes so that the butter can soften a bit and beome pliable. On a lightly floured surface, with a lightly floured rolling pin, roll the dough out into a rectangle that's about 8 x 15 inches, with a short side facing you. Start by pressing the dough down with the rolling pin, then roll.

Fold the top third of the dough rectangle down over the center and the bottom third up over that. Rotate the dough so the folded edge is to the left. Use a bench scraper to help lift and fold the dough if necessary. At this point, the dough will be rough and shaggy, with visible butter pieces, but as you continue to roll and fold it, it will come together. Repeat this rolling, folding, and turning process two more times, dusting the work surface, your hands, and the rolling pin with flour as necessary. What you have will not look like a cohesive dough for at least a couple of turns. Don't worry! Use the bench scraper to lift the crumbly dough up over itself for the first few folds. It will come together eventually. I promise. If the dough starts to fight you and become difficult to roll at any point, just pop it into the fridge for an extra rest.

Wrap the dough in plastic wrap and refrigerate for at least 1 hour.

Repeat the entire rolling and folding process three more times, for a grand total of six turns.

Wrap the dough well and refrigerate it for at least 2 hours, and up to overnight, before using.

For even rolling, the key is to make sure that the butter and the dough are the same temperature so that they roll out together. You don't want the butter to be so warm that it will be incorporated into the dough, but it must be soft enough to roll out.

The ideal rising temperature for a dough so loaded with butter is only about 70°F. Keep that in mind when you use this dough in any of the recipes in this book, or all those layers of butter you worked to create will ooze out before your pastries even make it to the oven.

Carrot Cake Buns

MAKES 12 BUNS

Carrot cake, but make it breakfast. Carrots not only flavor the fluffy orange dough, but also add sweetness and moisture. The spiced cream cheese swirl is only lightly sweetened, so you won't have any problem eating more than one.

To serve these buns for breakfast without having to get up at 2 a.m. to bake them, start them the day before. Let the buns rise until they've almost completed the second rise (about 20 minutes), then cover them lightly with plastic wrap and refrigerate overnight. About 1 hour before you'd like breakfast, take the buns out of the refrigerator and let them stand at room temperature until they have warmed up and fully risen, then bake and serve.

DOUGH

- ⅓ cup (80 grams) whole milk, warmed to 110°F
- ¼ cup (50 grams) granulated sugar, plus more for the pan
- 1½ teaspoons active dry yeast
- 1 cup (95 grams) finely shredded peeled carrot
- ½ cup (75 grams) golden raisins
- 2 large eggs (100 grams)
- 2½ cups (340 grams) bread flour, plus more for rolling
- ½ teaspoon kosher salt
- 6 tablespoons (¾ stick; 85 grams) butter, at room temperature, plus more for the baking dish

FILLING

- 4 ounces (113 grams) cream cheese, at room temperature
- ½ cup (57 grams) confectioners' sugar

- 1 teaspoon ground cinnamon
- 1 teaspoon ground ginger
- ½ teaspoon freshly grated nutmeg
- 1 large (20 grams) egg yolk

TO FINISH

- 1 large (50 grams) egg, lightly beaten
- Sanding sugar for sprinkling (optional)

You can shred the carrot on a box grater or throw it into the food processor. Either way will be just fine.

The butter should be at room temperature but not too soft. If you add super-soft butter to this dough, it will look too loose, and you may be tempted to add more flour—which would only lead to tough buns.

PREPARE THE DOUGH. In the bowl of a stand mixer fitted with the dough hook, combine the milk, 1 teaspoon of the sugar, and the

yeast and mix together. Let stand until foamy, about 5 minutes.

Add the remaining sugar, the carrot, raisins, eggs, flour, and salt to the bowl and knead on low speed until the dough starts to come together, about 3 minutes. Add the butter a little bit at a time and then continue to knead until the dough is smooth and elastic, another 3 to 4 minutes. (You can also make this dough by hand. When it comes time to add the butter, use a bench scraper to help lift the sticky dough up over itself as you knead with the other hand.)

Remove the bowl from the mixer stand, shape the dough into a tight ball in the bowl, and cover with plastic wrap. Let rise until it has doubled in size.

MEANWHILE, PREPARE THE FILLING. In a small bowl, mix together the cream cheese, confectioners' sugar, cinnamon, ginger, nutmeg, and egg yolk. Cover and set aside. (Chill the mixture if your house is warm.

continues

The filling should be spreadable but not super-soft.)

Butter an oven-safe skillet or a 9 x 2-inch round cake pan and sprinkle with granulated sugar.

When the dough has doubled, tip it out onto a very lightly floured surface and roll it into a 10-inch square. Spread the filling evenly over the surface. Tightly roll up the dough and pinch the seam closed. With a serrated knife, cut the roll crosswise into 12 pieces. Set the rounds in the prepared pan, spirals facing upward.

Cover the pan loosely with plastic wrap and let the buns rest until they have almost doubled in size, about 30 minutes.

Preheat the oven to 350°F.

Lightly brush the tops of the buns with the beaten egg. Sprinkle with the sanding sugar, if using. Bake until the buns are deep golden brown and set, 28 to 32 minutes. Let cool on a rack for at least 10 minutes before serving.

These are best the day they're made, but you can store leftovers in an airtight container at room temperature. Wrap them in foil and warm them in a toaster oven before serving.

To cut neat buns without spillage and smooshage, you can also use unflavored dental floss: Slide a piece of floss under one end of the log, then cross the ends of the floss up and over the log and pull on its ends to cut the first piece; repeat with the remaining dough.

Apricot Cardamom Buns

Swedish cardamom buns make a cozy nest for plump dried apricots.

DOUGH

- 1 recipe Basic Enriched Sweet Dough (page 179), prepared through the kneading step
- 1 teaspoon cardamom seeds, crushed
- ¾ cup (132 grams) chopped dried apricots

FILLING

- 6 tablespoons (¾ stick; 85 grams) butter, at room temperature
- 2 tablespoons (25 grams) dark brown sugar
- 2 teaspoons cardamom seeds, crushed
- Flour for rolling

TO FINISH

- 1 large (50 grams) egg, lightly beaten
- Pearl sugar for sprinkling (optional)
- ¼ cup (60 grams) apricot jam
- 1 tablespoon (15 grams) water

Plump and moist, Turkish apricots are my favorite for baking.

You want to use whole cardamom seeds here, not the finely ground stuff you find in bottles. Look for cardamom pods that are fresh and green, then use a mortar and pestle to bash the pods and remove the seeds. From there, you can pound the seeds to the correct consistency.

Swedish pearl sugar's bright white, coarse grains sit happily on top of these buns, even after baking. You don't need them, but they look cute and add a nice crunch. Sanding sugar also works nicely here.

PREPARE THE DOUGH. Add the cardamom and apricots to the dough and knead a few more times to incorporate. Continue through the first and second rises as directed in the recipe for Basic Enriched Sweet Dough.

PREPARE THE FILLING. In a small bowl, mix together the butter, sugar, and cardamom.

Line two baking sheets with parchment paper. On a lightly floured surface, roll the dough out into a 12 x 20-inch rectangle, with a short side facing you.

Spread the filling evenly over the surface. Fold the top third of the dough down over the center and the bottom third up over that.

Cut the dough lengthwise into 24 equal strips, about ½ inch wide. Take two strips and pinch them together at one end. Hold the pinched end in one hand and use the other hand to roll and twist the two strips together. Then coil the twisted strips into a round toward the pinched end and tuck the ends under. Transfer to one of the prepared baking sheets. Repeat with the remaining pieces of dough to make 12 rounds total, 6 per baking sheet.

Cover the sheets lightly with plastic wrap and allow the buns to puff, about 30 minutes.

Preheat the oven to 400°F.

Brush the buns with the beaten egg and sprinkle with pearl sugar, if using. Bake until puffed and deep golden, about 12 minutes. Meanwhile, in a small bowl, mix the apricot jam with the water; set aside.

Remove the buns from the oven, brush with the apricot syrup, and serve warm. These are best the day they're made.

Chocolate Sesame Swirl Bread

MAKES 1 LARGE LOAF

Halva is a sweet, flaky confection, most often made from sesame seeds. The best halva will melt in your mouth, and it is heavenly sprinkled over ice cream or yogurt, added to fruit crisps and cobblers, or baked into the dough for cookies and enriched breads.

FILLING

- ½ cup (150 grams) tahini
- ¼ cup (28 grams) confectioners' sugar
- 1½ teaspoons pure vanilla extract
- ½ teaspoon kosher salt
- ¾ cup (105 grams) bittersweet chocolate, melted
- 3½ ounces (99 grams) halva, coarsely chopped (about ¾ cup)

DOUGH

- Butter for the pan
- Flour for rolling
- 1 recipe Basic Enriched Sweet Dough (page 179)
- 1 large (50 grams) egg
- 1 tablespoon (15 grams) heavy cream

Tahini separates in the fridge. Stir it well or use an immersion blender to emulsify it before measuring.

PREPARE THE FILLING. In a small bowl, stir together the tahini, confectioners' sugar, vanilla, and salt. (It may seize up a bit. Don't worry. As long as it's spreadable, it's fine.)

PREPARE THE DOUGH. Butter an 8-inch springform pan. On a lightly floured surface, roll the dough out to a 14 x 16-inch rectangle, with a long edge parallel with the edge of the work surface. Spread the tahini mixture evenly over the dough. Drizzle the chocolate evenly over the tahini mixture. Sprinkle with the halva.

Cut the dough lengthwise in half, then cut each piece crosswise in half, to make 4 equal rectangles. Roll the first rectangle up into a coil, starting from the bottom. Set that coil on the bottom of the second rectangle and roll that rectangle up over the first one. Repeat with the remaining 2 rectangles. Transfer the coil to the prepared pan, cut side up. The process is a bit messy and you may lose a little bit of filling. Don't worry.

Cover the bread lightly with plastic wrap and set aside to rise for 30 minutes to 1 hour. The dough should puff and almost double in size.

Preheat the oven to 375°F.

Whisk together the egg and heavy cream. Remove the plastic and gently brush the coil with the egg wash. Bake until the coil is puffed, golden brown, and cooked through, 35 to 45 minutes. Tent with foil if it browns too quickly. The internal temperature should reach 190°F.

Transfer the pan to a rack and let the loaf cool for 20 minutes, then remove the sides of the pan. Serve the bread warm or at room temperature, cut into wedges.

This bread is best the day it's made, but you can store leftover slices in an airtight container at room temperature. Wrap them in foil and warm in a toaster oven before serving.

Shape this bread as directed, or shape it into a braided loaf like babka. You could even use the dough for buns, shaped like the Carrot Cake Buns on page 181.

Cinnamon Swirl Potato Bread

MAKES 2 LOAVES

Artie, my son, and I made this bread on an episode of our Food52 *series,* Cook and a Half. *I love it so much that I wanted to share it with you too.*

This recipe makes two loaves because it's very little extra work to make two rather than just one, and the bread freezes beautifully.

- ¾ cup (180 grams) whole milk, heated to about 115°F, plus 2 teaspoons for the egg wash
- ¼ cup (50 grams) granulated sugar
- 2½ teaspoons active dry yeast
- 2 large (100 grams) eggs
- 1½ teaspoons kosher salt
- ¾ cup (135 grams) peeled, cooked, and mashed russet potato
- 4 cups (544 grams) all-purpose flour
- 8 tablespoons (1 stick; 113 grams) butter, at room temperature, plus more for the pan
- ½ cup (100 grams) packed light brown sugar
- 2 tablespoons (8 grams) ground cinnamon

The mashed potato adds tenderness and increases the shelf life of this bread.

Filled rolled loaves tend to gape a bit, as the steam created in the oven gets trapped in the spiral. It's true that may be a bit unsightly, but it really doesn't affect the taste of the bread. Just slice, eat, and enjoy.

In the bowl of a mixer fitted with the dough hook, gently stir together the milk, 1 teaspoon of the granulated sugar, and the yeast. Let stand until foamy, about 5 minutes.

Separate one of the eggs and add the egg yolk, whole egg, salt, potato, flour, and the remaining granulated sugar to the yeast mixture. Mix on low speed until the dough starts to come together, about 3 minutes. It will still look a little bit dry; don't worry.

Still mixing on low, add the butter a piece or two at a time. At first it may look like it's not getting in there, but, it will; just keep adding and kneading. (You might have to stop the mixer and knead the butter in with your hands for a minute to get it started.) Once all the butter is incorporated, increase the speed to medium and knead the dough for another few minutes, until it is smooth and elastic.

Remove the bowl from the mixer stand, form the dough into a ball, cover the bowl with a towel, and set aside until doubled in size. This could take from 30 minutes to 2 hours, depending on how warm your house is. It's best to watch the dough rather than the clock.

Butter two 8½ x 4½-inch loaf pans and line them with parchment paper, leaving a 2-inch overhang on the two long sides. In a small bowl, combine the brown sugar and cinnamon. Cover and set aside.

Tip the dough out onto a work surface (you shouldn't need any flour at this point). Divide the dough in half. Keep one half covered while you work with the other. Pat or roll the dough out into an 8 x 14-inch rectangle. Sprinkle half of the brown sugar mixture evenly over the dough. Starting at one of the short ends, roll the dough up tightly and pinch the seam to seal. Set the loaf seam side down in one of the prepared pans. Repeat with the remaining dough and filling.

Cover the loaves and set aside to rise. They are ready to bake once the dough comes up to about 1 inch above the edges of the pans. Start preheating the oven to 350°F once the dough is about ½ inch above the edges of the pans.

Whisk the reserved egg white with the 2 teaspoons milk and gently brush over the tops of the loaves. Bake until they are deep golden brown and the internal temperature has reached 190°F, 30 to 35 minutes.

Let the loaves cool in the pans on a wire rack for 20 minutes, then tip the loaves out of the pans and turn right side up to cool completely before slicing.

Wrap completely cooled loaves in plastic wrap and store at room temperature for up to 3 days or freeze for up to 1 month. I like to toast slices straight from the freezer.

Ginger Brûlée Doughnuts

MAKES ABOUT 12 SMALL DOUGHNUTS

The Doughnut Plant, a wonderful shop in New York City, sells the most perfect crème brûlée doughnuts: fluffy dough, luscious vanilla bean–flecked custard, and a crunchy cap of shatter-ready caramel. In the past, I used to dip my custard-filled doughnuts in caramel for a brûlée effect, but after eating one at the Doughnut Plant, I realized that my version was missing that signature burnt sugar flavor. I took a note from them, pulled out my kitchen torch, and here we are.

GINGER CUSTARD

- 2 cups (480 grams) whole milk
- ¼ cup (45 grams) thinly sliced fresh ginger (not peeled)
- ¼ cup (50 grams) granulated sugar
- ¼ cup (32 grams) cornstarch
  Pinch of kosher salt
- 4 large (80 grams) egg yolks
- 2 tablespoons (¼ stick; 28 grams) butter
- ¼ cup (58 grams) heavy cream, whipped to soft peaks

DOUGH

- Flour for dusting and rolling
- 1 recipe Basic Enriched Sweet Dough (page 179), prepared through the first rise and chilled
- Neutral oil for deep-frying

TO FINISH

- Superfine sugar for dipping

Cold dough is much easier to shape and cut. After the first rise, wrap the dough well and set it in the fridge for at least an hour.

The ginger is added off the heat to prevent curdling.

Keeping the oil at the correct temperature by adjusting the heat occasionally as necessary is important for properly cooked doughnuts. If the oil is not hot enough, the doughnuts will absorb too much oil. If it's too hot, the outsides will get too dark and crisp before the insides are cooked through. I highly recommend using a deep-fry/candy thermometer, but if you don't have one, throw a few pinches of flour into the oil to check the temperature. If the flour sizzles, the oil is ready.

PREPARE THE GINGER CUSTARD. In a medium saucepan, heat the milk over medium-high heat until hot, but don't let it simmer. Immediately remove the pan from the heat. Add the ginger, cover, and let stand for at least 20 minutes, or longer for a deeper ginger flavor. Strain out the ginger.

In a medium bowl, whisk together the sugar, cornstarch, salt, and egg yolks. Whisk in about ½ cup of the ginger milk, a little bit at a time to prevent lumps, then return the mixture to the saucepan.

Add the butter to the pan, bring to a boil over medium heat, whisking constantly, and boil for 2 minutes. Remove the pan from the heat and immediately pour the custard through a fine-mesh sieve into a bowl. Cover the custard with plastic wrap or wax paper pressed directly against the surface of the custard and transfer to the fridge to cool completely.

PREPARE THE DOUGH. Line two baking sheets with clean dish towels or parchment paper. Dust well with flour. Tip the cold dough out onto a lightly floured work surface and roll out to about ½ inch thick. Using a 2¼-inch round cutter, cut out 12 doughnuts and transfer 6 to each prepared sheet. Lightly cover with plastic wrap and set in a warm place to double in size, about 30 minutes to an hour.

When you're ready to fry, line a rimmed baking sheet with paper towels. Pour about 2 inches of oil into a medium heavy-bottomed pot. Attach a deep-fry/candy thermometer to the side of the pot and heat the oil to 350°F.

Add 2 to 3 doughnuts to the oil and fry, turning once, for 2 to 3 minutes per side, until golden brown. Using the slotted spoon, transfer to the paper towels to cool. Repeat with the remaining rounds of dough.

To fill the doughnuts, use the handle of a wooden spoon to poke a hole into one side of each doughnut, being careful not to poke it through the other side.

Whisk the chilled ginger cream to loosen it, then fold in the whipped cream. Transfer the cream mixture to a pastry bag fitted with a small round tip. One at a time, insert the pastry tip into each doughnut and gently squeeze the bag to fill the doughnuts.

Set the superfine sugar in a shallow bowl. Dip the top of each doughnut into the sugar and transfer to a baking sheet. Run a kitchen torch over the top of each doughnut to caramelize the sugar. Then dip and caramelize the doughnuts a few more times, until you have a nice, crunchy sugar top. Serve immediately.

These doughnuts are best the day they're made.

Marmalade Blueberry Bread

MAKES 1 LOAF

Bittersweet marmalade and wild blueberries combine to make a delightful filling with scarcely any work.

1 recipe Basic Enriched Sweet Dough (page 179), prepared through the first rise

½ cup (160 grams) orange marmalade, plus more for brushing

1½ teaspoons ground cinnamon

¾ cup (113 grams) small blueberries, preferably wild

1 large (50 grams) egg, lightly beaten

Sanding sugar for sprinkling

Small wild blueberries are packed with bright blueberry flavor, but they are hard to find fresh. Thankfully, frozen wild blueberries have now found their way to most larger grocery stores. Before using them here, set them on a paper towel to thaw. The paper towel will absorb some of the released juices that would otherwise sog out your bread.

Tip the risen dough out onto a work surface. Roll or pat it into a 10-inch square. Spread the marmalade evenly over the surface and sprinkle with the cinnamon and blueberries. Tightly roll up the dough and pinch the seam closed.

With a serrated knife, cut the roll lengthwise down the center. Cross the two halves over and around each other, cut side up, then wrap one end around to the other and pinch the ends together. Transfer to the pan with the topping cut side up. Cover loosely with plastic wrap and let rise until the dough has puffed and jiggles when shaken gently.

Preheat the oven to 350°F.

Uncover, brush the dough with the beaten egg, and sprinkle with sanding sugar. Bake the bread until deep golden brown and puffed, 45 to 50 minutes; the internal temperature should be 190°F. Tent the bread with foil if it darkens before it is cooked through.

Transfer the pan to a rack and let cool for 15 minutes. Then tip the bread out, set it right side up on the rack, and brush with more marmalade. Let cool slightly before slicing.

Store leftovers in an airtight container at room temperature for up to 3 days, or freeze for up to 1 month.

Roulés aux Raisins with Pistachio Cream

There are a lot of components required to create these pastries, but all of them can be made in advance, and I promise it's well worth it. The rolls are buttery, crisp, and creamy in all the right places.

Softened butter for the ring molds

Superfine sugar for the English muffin rings and for dipping and sprinkling

3   tablespoons (18 grams) Nut Paste (page 151) made with pistachios

2   tablespoons (16 grams) finely chopped pistachios

¼   teaspoon pure almond extract

½   recipe Basic Custard (page 94)

Flour for rolling

1   recipe Rough Laminated Yeasted Dough (page 180), allowed to rest overnight in the refrigerator

1   cup (160 grams) golden raisins

1   large (50 grams) egg, whisked

English muffin rings are just short ring molds. You can find them at any cooking supply store or online. If you don't have them, bake the rolls in a very well-greased muffin tin, and don't sugar the bottoms of the pastries. They won't look the same, but they will taste just as good.

Butter ten 3½-inch English muffin rings and sprinkle the sides with superfine sugar. Line two rimmed baking sheets with parchment paper and arrange 5 rings on each sheet.

Stir the pistachio paste, chopped pistachios, and almond extract into the custard.

On a lightly floured surface, roll the dough out to a 9 x 20-inch rectangle. Trim the edges to make a neat rectangle (but don't trim off too much!).

Spread the custard evenly over the dough. Sprinkle evenly with the raisins. Starting from a long side, roll the dough up tightly and pinch the seam to seal.

Use a serrated knife to cut the dough into 10 equal pieces. Tap the bottom of each roll in superfine sugar, then place the rolls in the prepared ring mold. Tuck any exposed raisins into the dough so they don't burn in the oven. Cover the rolls lightly with plastic wrap and let rise until puffed, about 30 minutes.

Preheat the oven to 375°F, with the racks in the upper and lower thirds of the oven.

Gently brush each roll with the whisked egg and sprinkle with superfine sugar. Bake the rolls until they are puffed and deeply golden brown, 25 to 30 minutes, rotating the sheets halfway through. Transfer to racks to cool slightly, but remove the rings while the pastries are still warm. Serve warm or at room temperature.

These are best the day they're made.

Cover the pastries with foil if they start to brown too quickly in the oven.

Rhubarb and Cheese Kolaches

MAKES 12 PASTRIES

Kolaches are soft, fluffy Czech pastries that are usually filled with fruit and topped with a sugary crumble. I ate my first one only recently, on a trip to Texas, but I haven't been able to get them out of my head. I hope you feel the same way.

DOUGH

- ½ cup (120 grams) whole milk, warmed to 110°F to 120°F
- 2¼ teaspoons active dry yeast (one 7 gram package)
- 1 tablespoon (13 grams) granulated sugar
- 2¾ cups (374 grams) all-purpose flour
- 10 tablespoons (1¼ sticks; 141 grams) butter, melted
- 2 large (100 grams) eggs
- 1 large (20 grams) egg yolk
- ¾ teaspoon kosher salt

CHEESE FILLING

- 8 ounces (226 grams) cream cheese, at room temperature
- 3 tablespoons (23 grams) confectioners' sugar
- 1 large (20 grams) egg yolk
- 1 teaspoon finely grated lemon zest

RHUBARB

- 1¾ cups (200 grams) diced rhubarb
- ¼ cup (50 grams) granulated sugar
- ½ vanilla bean, split lengthwise and seeds scraped out and reserved
- ½ teaspoon finely grated lemon zest
- 2 teaspoons cornstarch

CRUMBLE

- 3 tablespoons (26 grams) all-purpose flour
- 2 tablespoons (25 grams) granulated sugar
- 2 tablespoons (¼ stick; 28 grams) butter, melted
- ½ teaspoon ground cinnamon
- Pinch of kosher salt

TO FINISH

- 1 large (50 grams) egg, lightly beaten

Because fresh rhubarb breaks down quickly when cooked, freezing it, which breaks down the fruit's cell walls, doesn't make much of a difference at all. I like to buy a big bunch of rhubarb when it's in season, wash and dice it, and then pop it into the freezer for whenever the mood strikes.

PREPARE THE DOUGH. In the bowl of a stand mixer fitted with the dough hook, combine the milk, yeast, and a pinch of the sugar and let stand until foamy, about 3 minutes.

Add the remaining sugar, the flour, butter, eggs, egg yolk, and salt to the yeast mixture and knead on medium speed until you have a smooth, supple dough. It will look too wet at first, but don't worry—it will come together and clear the sides of the bowl eventually; don't be tempted to add more flour.

Scrape down the sides of the bowl, form the dough into a ball, and cover with plastic wrap. Let the dough double in size. This could take up to 2 hours; keep an eye on the dough rather than the clock. (At this point, instead of letting the dough rise at room temperature, you can also let it proof in the fridge, well wrapped, overnight.)

PREPARE THE CHEESE FILLING. In a medium bowl, stir together the cream cheese, confectioners' sugar, egg yolk, and lemon zest.

PREPARE THE RHUBARB. In a small saucepan, combine the rhubarb, sugar, vanilla bean seeds, lemon zest, and cornstarch and cook over medium heat, stirring often, until the rhubarb has softened and the mixture has bubbled and thickened, about 5 minutes. Cool completely.

continues

PREPARE THE CRUMBLE. In a small bowl, combine the flour, sugar, butter, cinnamon, and salt and mix together with a fork.

When the dough has risen, line a 13 x 9-inch baking pan with parchment paper. Tip the dough out and cut it into 12 equal pieces. (You shouldn't need flour at this point.) Roll one piece of dough into a tight ball by setting it on a work surface, cupping your hand over it, and circling it over and over again, adding a little pressure with your palm. Transfer the ball to the prepared pan and repeat with the remaining dough.

Cover the balls and set aside until puffed, about 30 minutes.

Preheat the oven to 375°F.

Use your fingers to gently press an indentation into the center of each ball. Brush the balls with the beaten egg. Fill each indentation with some of the cream cheese mixture, then top with the rhubarb. Sprinkle the crumble evenly over each kolache.

Bake the kolaches until puffed, set, and golden brown in spots, 20 to 25 minutes. Transfer to a rack to cool. Serve warm or at room temperature.

These are best the day they're made, but you can store leftovers in an airtight container at room temperature. Wrap them in foil and warm them in a toaster oven before serving.

Pretzel Cheese Buns

I use the same soft dough for these buns as for the kolaches on page 196. These buns are softer and doughier than classic pretzels, in the best way.

DOUGH

- ½ cup (120 grams) whole milk, warmed to 110°F to 120°F
- 2¼ teaspoons active dry yeast (one 7 gram package)
- 1 tablespoon (13 grams) granulated sugar
- 2¾ cups (374 grams) all-purpose flour
- 10 tablespoons (1¼ sticks; 141 grams) butter, melted
- 2 large (100 grams) eggs
- 1 large (20 grams) egg yolk
- ¾ teaspoon kosher salt

FILLING

- 6 ounces (170 grams) cream cheese, at room temperature
- 1 cup (85 grams) shredded cheddar
- 2 tablespoons (30 grams) grainy mustard
- 1 large (20 grams) egg yolk
- ½ cup (30 grams) sliced fresh chives

WATER BATH

- 8 cups (2 kilograms) water
- ⅓ cup (85 grams) baking soda
- 3 tablespoons (38 grams) dark brown sugar

TO FINISH

- Kosher salt, pretzel salt, or flaky salt for sprinkling

Traditional pretzels are dipped in a lye solution before baking, which gives them their signature brown color and tangy flavor. But lye is dangerous to work with. Dipping these pretzels in a baking soda and brown sugar solution does a similar job without the danger.

PREPARE THE DOUGH. In the bowl of a stand mixer fitted with the dough hook, combine the milk, yeast, and a pinch of the sugar and let stand until foamy, about 3 minutes.

Add the remaining sugar, the flour, butter, eggs, egg yolk, and salt to the yeast mixture and knead on medium until you have a smooth, supple dough, about 4 minutes. It will look too wet at first, but don't worry—it will come together and clear the sides of the bowl eventually; don't be tempted to add more flour.

Scrape down the sides of the bowl, form the dough into a ball, and cover with plastic wrap. Let the dough double in size. This could take up to 2 hours; keep an eye on the dough rather than the clock. (At this point, instead of letting the dough rise at room temperature, you could instead let it proof in the fridge, well wrapped, overnight.)

PREPARE THE FILLING. In the bowl of a food processor, combine the cream cheese, cheddar, mustard, and egg yolk and process until smooth. Transfer to a bowl and fold in the chives.

Line a rimmed baking sheet with parchment paper. Tip the dough out and cut it into 12 equal pieces. (You shouldn't need flour at this point.) Roll one piece of dough into a tight ball by setting it on a work surface, cupping your hand over it, and circling it over and over again, adding a little pressure with your palm. Transfer the ball to the prepared sheet and repeat with the remaining dough. Cover with plastic wrap and set aside until the balls are puffed, about 30 minutes.

Preheat the oven to 375°F.

Use your fingers to gently press an indentation into the center of each ball of dough.

PREPARE THE WATER BATH. Bring the water to a simmer in

continues

a large pot. (Make sure the pot is deep enough that the water remains at least a few inches below the rim, as it will bubble furiously when you add the baking soda.) Add the baking soda and brown sugar to the water and whisk to combine.

Once the bubbles have mostly subsided, carefully add 2 to 3 balls of dough to the pot. Cook, turning once, for 15 seconds per side, then use a spider or slotted spoon to transfer them back to the prepared sheet. Sprinkle with salt. Repeat with the remaining buns. The buns will look deflated and a little wrinkly when they come out of the baking soda solution, but they will puff back up in the oven.

Fill the indentations in the buns with the cream cheese mixture. Bake until the buns are puffed, set, and golden brown in spots, 20 to 24 minutes. Transfer to a rack to cool. Serve the buns warm or at room temperature.

These are best the day they're made, but you can store leftovers in an airtight container at room temperature. Wrap them in foil and warm them in a toaster oven before serving.

If your pot is very large, double the water bath mixture.

Raspberry and Almond Bear Claws

These are reminiscent of almond croissants, but with a dollop of raspberry jam, they are even lovelier. We took to calling these bear claws "Giselle" during the photo shoot because they were just so pretty and always knew how to find their light.

1 recipe Rough Laminated Yeasted Dough (page 180)

Flour for rolling

½ recipe Nut Paste (page 151) made with almonds

½ cup (160 grams) raspberry jam

1 large (50 grams) egg, lightly beaten

GLAZE (OPTIONAL)

1 cup (120 grams) confectioners' sugar, sifted

1 tablespoon (15 grams) whole milk

½ teaspoon pure vanilla extract

Sliced almonds for sprinkling

Line two rimmed baking sheets with parchment paper. Tip the dough out and cut it in half. Return one half to the fridge. On a lightly floured surface, roll one piece of dough into a 12-inch square. Trim the edges to even them.

Roll half of the almond paste out into a 12 x 4-inch rectangle. Place the almond paste on the left half of the dough square. Spread ¼ cup of the jam over the almond paste. Fold the left third of the dough over the center, then fold the right third over that, like a business letter. Now you have a 12 x 4-inch rectangle. Fold the dough lengthwise in half, so you have a 12 x 2-inch rectangle. Cut the dough into six 2-inch squares and transfer them to one of the prepared baking sheets. Repeat with the remaining dough, almond paste, and jam and transfer to the second sheet.

Make 4 cuts through each pastry, from left to right, leaving the top side of it intact. They will look like squat combs with four thick bristles each. Cover lightly with plastic wrap and let stand at room temperature until puffed, about 45 minutes.

Preheat the oven to 400°F, with the racks in the upper and lower thirds of the oven.

Carefully brush the bear claws with the beaten egg.

Bake until the claws are puffed and golden brown, 18 to 22 minutes, rotating the sheets halfway through. Transfer to a rack to cool completely.

PREPARE THE OPTIONAL GLAZE. In a small bowl, whisk together the confectioners' sugar, milk, and vanilla until smooth. Drizzle the glaze over the cooled claws. Sprinkle with the almonds.

These are best the day they're made.

It's very important to keep the dough cool while rolling it out and proofing the pastries so that none of the butter seeps out. Chill them after shaping if the butter has gotten warm. And make sure the ambient temperature is only about 70°F for proofing.

Sticky Banana Monkey Bread

SERVES 8 TO 10

This recipe, with its numerous dough balls that need dipping, is a great one for little helpers.

DOUGH

- ½ cup (120 grams) whole milk, warmed to 110°F to 120°F
- 2¼ teaspoons active dry yeast (one 7 gram package)
- ¼ cup (50 grams) granulated sugar
- 3½ cups (476 grams) all-purpose flour
- 1 cup (220 grams) mashed overripe banana
- 1 large (50 grams) egg, at room temperature
- 1 teaspoon kosher salt
- 6 tablespoons (¾ stick; 85 grams) butter, at room temperature, plus more for the pan

COATING

- 1½ cups (300 grams) packed light brown sugar
- 1 tablespoon (4 grams) ground cinnamon
- 8 tablespoons (1 stick; 113 grams) butter, melted

GLAZE

- 4 ounces (113 grams) cream cheese, at room temperature
- 1 tablespoon (8 grams) confectioners' sugar
- 1 to 2 tablespoons (15 to 30 grams) milk, warmed
- 1 tablespoon (15 grams) bourbon

PREPARE THE DOUGH. In the bowl of a stand mixer fitted with the dough hook, stir together the milk, yeast, and 1 teaspoon of the sugar. Let stand until foamy, about 5 minutes.

Add the remaining sugar and the flour to the yeast mixture. With the mixer on low speed, mix in the banana, egg, and salt, until the dough forms and it becomes elastic, about 5 minutes. Add the butter a bit at a time, mixing until it is incorporated, and then knead the dough until it is smooth, another 5 minutes or so. The dough will be sticky, but resist the urge to add more flour.

Scrape down the sides of the bowl, remove the bowl from the mixer stand, and shape the dough into a neat ball. Cover with plastic wrap and set aside in a warm place to rise until doubled, 1 to 2 hours, depending on the temperature of your kitchen. (After the dough has doubled, you can also punch it down, wrap it well, and refrigerate for up to 2 days before proceeding.)

Using a pastry brush, generously butter a 12-cup Bundt pan.

PREPARE THE COATING. In a small bowl, mix together the brown sugar and cinnamon. Put the melted butter in another small bowl.

Pat the dough out into a large square. Using a large knife or a pastry wheel, cut it into 36 equal pieces. Roll one piece of dough into a ball, dip it in the butter, toss lightly in the sugar mixture, and place in the prepared pan. Repeat with the remaining dough, stacking the balls on top of one another in the pan.

Cover the pan lightly with plastic wrap and set aside until the dough has puffed and jiggles when shaken gently, about 1 hour.

Preheat the oven to 350°F.

Uncover the pan and bake the bread until it's puffed and set, about 35 minutes. An instant-read thermometer inserted into the center should read at least 190°F. Immediately and carefully flip the bread out onto a plate. Let cool slightly.

MEANWHILE, PREPARE THE GLAZE. In a small bowl, whisk together the cream cheese, confectioners' sugar, milk, and bourbon.

Drizzle the glaze over the bread. Serve warm or at room temperature.

Monkey bread is best the day it's made, but you can store leftovers in an airtight container at room temperature. Wrap them in foil and warm them in a toaster oven before serving.

A tube pan would also be fine here, but make sure it doesn't have a removable bottom, or it might leak.

Butterscotch Brioche Suisse

MAKES 10 BUNS

Brioche Suisse is a very special brioche-and-cream bun with chocolate. This one is filled with a luscious butterscotch custard.

BUTTERSCOTCH CUSTARD

- 6 tablespoons (75 grams) dark brown sugar
- 2 tablespoons (¼ stick; 28 grams) butter
- 1 cup (240 grams) whole milk, warmed
- 2½ tablespoons (20 grams) cornstarch
- 2 tablespoons (25 grams) granulated sugar
- Pinch of kosher salt
- 2 large (40 grams) egg yolks
- 1½ teaspoons pure vanilla extract

DOUGH

- Flour for rolling
- 1 recipe Basic Enriched Sweet Dough (page 179) prepared with 6 tablespoons (¾ stick; 85 grams) butter

TO FINISH

- ½ cup (70 grams) semisweet chocolate, chopped
- 1 large (50 grams) egg, lightly beaten

PREPARE THE BUTTERSCOTCH CUSTARD. In a medium saucepan, combine the brown sugar and butter and heat over medium heat, whisking, until the sugar melts, 1 to 2 minutes. Then cook, whisking constantly, until the mixture smoothes out and darkens a bit, about 3 minutes. Remove from the heat.

In a large glass measuring cup, whisk together the warm milk, cornstarch, granulated sugar, and salt. Pour the milk into the pot—the mixture will seize, but don't worry! Return the pot to the heat, and cook, whisking constantly, until the clumps of caramel melt and the mixture thickens, 4 to 5 minutes. Remove from the heat.

In a small bowl, whisk together some of the warm milk mixture and the egg yolks.

Set a fine-mesh sieve over the glass measuring cup.

Return the pot to medium heat and cook, whisking constantly, until the custard has just come to a very low boil, about 2 minutes. Immediately remove from the heat and pour the custard through the sieve into the measuring cup. Stir in the vanilla. Press plastic wrap or wax paper directly against the surface of the custard and refrigerate until cold.

PREPARE THE DOUGH. Line two rimmed baking sheets with parchment paper. On a lightly floured surface, roll the dough out into an 18 x 12-inch rectangle. Spread the cooled custard evenly over half of the dough. Sprinkle the chocolate over the custard. Fold the other half of the dough over the custard, so that you have an 18 x 6-inch rectangle. Cut the dough into 10 rectangles.

Transfer 5 rectangles to each prepared sheet. Cover lightly with plastic and let rise at room temperature until the buns have puffed up, about 45 minutes.

Preheat the oven to 350°F, with the racks in the upper and lower thirds of the oven.

Gently brush each bun with the beaten egg. Bake the buns until they are browned and set, about 15 minutes, rotating the sheets halfway through. Don't overbake, or the pastries will be dry. Transfer the buns to a rack to cool.

Serve warm or at room temperature.

These are best the day they're made, but you can store leftovers in an airtight container at room temperature. Wrap them in foil and warm them in a toaster oven before serving.

Try these with a thin layer of Nut Paste (page 151) tucked under the custard.

Earl Grey Cream Danish Buns

MAKES 9 BUNS

These buns are a cross between a cream puff and a doughnut, with the flake of a good croissant. They're filled with an Earl Grey–flavored cream that makes me think of the perfect cup of milky sweet tea.

EARL GREY CREAM

- ¾ cup (180 grams) heavy cream
- ¾ cup (180 grams) whole milk
- 3 Earl Grey tea bags or about 1 tablespoon (5 grams) loose tea
- 1 large (50 grams) egg
- 3 large (60 grams) egg yolks
- 1 tablespoon (8 grams) cornstarch
- ¼ cup (50 grams) granulated sugar

DOUGH

- Flour for rolling
- 1 recipe Rough Laminated Yeasted Dough (page 180), allowed to rest overnight in the refrigerator

TO FINISH

- 1 large (50 grams) egg, lightly beaten
- Granulated sugar for sprinkling
- ¾ cup (105 grams) semisweet chocolate, melted

PREPARE THE EARL GREY CREAM. In a medium pot, bring the cream and milk to a boil. Remove from the heat and add the tea bags or loose tea. Set aside to steep for at least 20 minutes.

If using tea bags, squeeze them into the cream and discard them. Transfer the cream to a large glass measuring cup. If using loose tea, pour the mixture through a fine mesh sieve set over a large glass measuring cup. Press the tea into the sieve to extract all the cream.

Add the egg, egg yolks, cornstarch, and sugar to the pot and whisk together. Add the cream mixture and whisk to combine.

Set a fine-mesh sieve over the measuring cup. Heat the cream mixture over medium heat, whisking constantly, until it begins to thicken, about 4 minutes. Remove from the heat and pour through the sieve into the measuring cup. (You should have about 1½ cups cream.)

Press plastic wrap or wax paper directly against the surface of the cream and chill until cold, at least 2 hours.

PREPARE THE DOUGH. Line two rimmed baking sheets with parchment paper. On a lightly floured work surface, roll the dough out into a 12¼-inch square. Trim ¼ inch off the edges to even them; discard the excess dough. Cut the dough into nine 4-inch squares.

Scoop about 2 tablespoons of the cream onto the center of each square. Bring the four corners of one square up into the center and press the edges to seal. Then bring the four corners up into the center again and press to seal. Roll the pastry into a ball and transfer to one of the parchment-lined baking sheets, seam side down. Repeat with the remaining squares and filling.

Cover the buns lightly with plastic wrap and let puff at room temperature, about 45 minutes.

Preheat the oven to 375°F, with the racks in the upper and lower thirds of the oven.

Carefully brush each bun with the beaten egg and sprinkle liberally with sugar. Bake until the buns are golden brown and set, about 15 minutes, rotating the sheets halfway through. Transfer the buns to racks to cool.

Drizzle the buns with the melted chocolate to serve.

These are best the day they're made, but you can store leftovers in an airtight container at room temperature. Wrap them in foil and warm them in a toaster oven before serving.

Shaping these pastries is a little tricky. The filling wants to ooze out. Try not to worry too much—you only need a little bit of the filling to flavor the finished bun.

Big, Fluffy Lemon and Orange Buns

My wonderful ex-mother-in-law makes very similar orange buns every Christmas for everyone she loves. I think her ability to share them is a holiday miracle. When I make these, I keep them all for myself. Just kidding. Kind of.

DOUGH

- ⅔ cup (160 grams) whole milk, warmed to 110°F to 120°F
- 2 teaspoons active dry yeast
- 3 tablespoons (38 grams) granulated sugar
- 2½ cups (340 grams) all-purpose flour
- ½ teaspoon kosher salt
- 1 large (50 grams) egg, at room temperature
- 6 tablespoons (¾ stick; 85 grams) butter, at room temperature

FILLING

- 3 tablespoons (15 grams) finely grated orange zest (from about 2 navel oranges)
- 2 tablespoons (6 grams) finely grated lemon zest (from about 2 large lemons)
- 6 tablespoons (75 grams) granulated sugar
- 3 tablespoons (⅜ stick; 42 grams) butter, at room temperature
- Pinch of kosher salt

GLAZE

- 4 ounces (113 grams) cream cheese, at room temperature
- 2 tablespoons (15 grams) confectioners' sugar
- 2 tablespoons (30 grams) warm milk

PREPARE THE DOUGH. In the bowl of a stand mixer fitted with the dough hook, combine the milk, yeast, and 1 teaspoon of the sugar. Let stand until foamy, about 5 minutes.

Add the remaining sugar, the flour, and salt to the yeast mixture. With the mixer on low speed, add the egg and mix until a dough forms and it becomes elastic, about 5 minutes. Add the butter a bit at a time, beating until it is all incorporated, and then continue to knead the dough until it is smooth, about 5 minutes. The dough will be sticky.

Remove the bowl from the mixer stand, scrape down the sides, and shape the dough into a neat ball. Cover with plastic wrap and set aside to rise in a warm place until doubled, 1 to 2 hours, depending on the temperature of your kitchen. (At this point, you can also punch the dough down, wrap it well, and refrigerate for up to 2 days. The cold dough will be easy to work with, but it will take a little longer to rise.)

PREPARE THE FILLING. In a small bowl, using your fingers, rub the orange zest and lemon zest into

the sugar to release some of the citrus oils. Add the butter and salt and mix until well combined.

Line a rimmed baking sheet with parchment paper. Tip the dough out and pat it into a 10-inch square. (You shouldn't need any flour at this point.) Spread the filling evenly over the dough. Cut the square into 8 equal strips. Roll each strip up and set it on the prepared sheet, swirl side up. You can keep the buns close together, leaving just about ¼ inch between them.

Cover the buns lightly with plastic wrap and let rise at room temperature until they have puffed up, about 45 minutes.

Preheat the oven to 350°F.

Bake the buns until they are browned and set, about 20 minutes. Transfer the baking sheet to a rack to cool slightly.

MEANWHILE, PREPARE THE GLAZE. In a small bowl, mix together the cream cheese, confectioners' sugar, and milk. Drizzle over the warm buns.

Serve the buns warm or at room temperature.

These are best the day they're made, but you can store leftovers in an airtight container at room temperature. Wrap them in foil and warm them in a toaster oven before serving.

If you bake these buns in a 9-inch square baking pan, they will be even squidgier.

Yeasted Coffee Cake with Pears

SERVES 12

Tender like a cake but with the subtle chew of an enriched bread, this yeasted coffee cake is the best of both worlds.

DOUGH

- ¾ cup (180 grams) whole milk, warmed to 110°F to 120°F
- 2¼ teaspoons active dry yeast (one 7 gram package)
- ¾ cup (150 grams) granulated sugar
- 3 cups (408 grams) all-purpose flour
- 8 tablespoons (1 stick; 113 grams) butter, melted and slightly cooled
- 1 large (50 grams) egg, at room temperature
- 1 large (20 grams) egg yolk, at room temperature
- 1½ teaspoons baking powder
- 1 teaspoon kosher salt

FILLING/TOPPING

- ¾ cup (150 grams) granulated sugar, plus 2 tablespoons (25 grams)
- 1 tablespoon (4 grams) ground cinnamon
- 2 teaspoons pure vanilla extract
- ½ cup (57 grams) chopped walnuts
- 4 medium-ripe pears, halved, cored, and thinly sliced
- 2 tablespoons (¼ stick; 28 grams) butter, cubed, plus more for the pan

GLAZE

- 1½ cups (180 grams) confectioners' sugar, sifted
- 1 tablespoon (15 grams) fresh lemon juice
- 1 to 2 tablespoons (15 to 30 grams) heavy cream

Look for pears that are ripe but not too soft. You want fruit that will keep its shape without releasing too much juice. Apples would be lovely here too.

PREPARE THE DOUGH. In the bowl of a stand mixer fitted with the dough hook, combine the milk, yeast, and a pinch of the sugar and let stand until foamy, about 3 minutes.

Add the remaining sugar, the flour, butter, egg, egg yolk, baking powder, and salt to the yeast mixture and mix until a dough forms and it becomes elastic, about 5 minutes. It will look too wet at first, but don't worry—it will come together and clear the sides of the bowl eventually. Don't be tempted to add more flour.

Remove the bowl from the mixer stand, scrape down the sides of the bowl, and form the dough into a ball. Cover with plastic wrap and let the dough double. This could take up to 2 hours, depending on the temperature of your kitchen. Keep an eye on the dough, rather than the clock. (At this point, instead of letting the dough rise at room temperature, you could let it proof in the fridge, well wrapped, for up to 2 days.)

PREPARE THE FILLING/TOPPING. In a medium bowl, combine the ¾ cup sugar, the cinnamon, vanilla, and walnuts. In another bowl, toss the pears with the remaining 2 tablespoons sugar.

Butter a 13 x 9-inch baking pan. Roll the dough out to a 13 x 18-inch rectangle. Sprinkle half of the filling over one half of the dough. Fold the other half of the dough over the filling so that you have a 13 x 9-inch rectangle.

Set the dough in the prepared pan. Top with the remaining filling and then fan the pears over it in a decorative pattern. Scatter the butter pieces over the top. Cover lightly with plastic wrap and let rise until the dough has puffed, about 45 minutes.

Preheat the oven to 350°F.

Bake the cake until puffed and golden brown in spots, 30 to 35 minutes. Transfer to a rack to cool slightly.

MEANWHILE, PREPARE THE GLAZE. In a small bowl, whisk together the sugar, lemon juice, and cream.

Drizzle the glaze over the warm cake. Serve warm or at room temperature.

This is best the day it's made, but you can store leftovers in an airtight container at room temperature. Wrap the squares in foil and warm in a toaster oven before serving.

Acknowledgments

My greatest joy is collaborating with all the brilliant people I'm lucky enough to know. I could never do what I do without the support of the team, and everything I make reflects that fact.

Laura Arnold, recipe tester extraordinaire, diligently worked her way through the recipes in this book, and every single one is better for it.

Johnny Miller captured the beauty in every swirl, dollop, and crumb with flair. I think his images are extraordinary and I'm so grateful for these and the hundreds of other shots he never seemed to tire of taking.

Ali Slagle, technically the prop stylist but also schmoo wrangler and thoughtful taster, was full of new perspectives and ideas on both the visuals and the recipes. (Shout-out to Ayca Kilicoglu of MÜR by Ayca for those gorgeous textiles.)

Eliza Winograd, Caroline Lange, and Fatima Khamise baked some of the most gorgeous food I've ever seen for the photos and even found time to fine-tune some of the recipes as we went along.

Thank you to Jenny Abramson; Shira Bocar; B Chatfield; Cate Conmy; Julia Gartland; Juliet Gorman; Cas Holman; Miriam Kasell; Amy Leo; Laura Rege; Sarah Rosenthal; Zayary Santos; Augustine Sedgewick; Lauryn Tyrell; and Artiebug; my mom, Suneetha; and my dad, Upali, for being my friends, my beloveds, my taste testers, and primo idea generators.

The wonderful team at HarperCollins—Sarah Kwak, Deb Brody, Tai Blanche, Rachel Meyers, Jill Lazer, Nick Smalls, and Katie Tull—helped me create a book I'm so proud of. My deepest thanks.

My agent, Janis Donnaud, believed in me first, and she continues to do so. I appreciate you, Janis.

And to all the cooks and bakers who've come before me, inspired these recipes, and taught me everything I know, thank you. I promise to pay it forward.

Index

HarperCollins books may be purchased for educational, business, or sales
promotional use. For information, please email the Special Markets Department
at SPsales@harpercollins.com.

FIRST EDITION

Designed by Tai Blanche
Photographs by Johnny Miller
Prop styling by Ali Slagle
Food stying by Fatima Khamise, Caroline Lange, Samantha Seneviratne,
and Eliza Winograd
MÜR patterns by Ayca Kilicoglu
Texture background © Shutterstock

Library of Congress Cataloging-in-Publication Data

Names: Seneviratne, Samantha, author.
Title: Bake smart : sweets and secrets from my oven to yours / Samantha
 Seneviratne.
Description: First edition. | New York : Harvest, an imprint of William
 Morrow, [2023] | Includes index.
Identifiers: LCCN 2023020173 | ISBN 9780358715146 (hardcover) | ISBN
 9780063307872 (ebook)
Subjects: LCSH: Baking. | LCGFT: Cookbooks.
Classification: LCC TX763 .S3968 2023 | DDC 641.81/5—dc23/eng/20230501
LC record available at https://lccn.loc.gov/2023020173

ISBN 978-0-358-71514-6

23 24 25 26 27 RTL 10 9 8 7 6 5 4 3 2 1